Kids guide TO THE TOKYO OLYMPICS

TOKYO 2020
TOKYO 2020

Kids guide TO THE TOKYO OLYMPICS

SportsEngine, a division of
NBC Sports Digital & Consumer Business
Minneapolis, MN

The author wishes to thank Megan Soisson, Sarah Hughes, Andrew Dougherty, and the rest of the NBC Sports Olympic researchers who provided invaluable fact-checking for hundreds of individual Olympic and historical facts. Without their support, this guide would not have been possible.

A special thanks to all of the United States Olympic and Paralympic Committee and the national governing bodies who provided content for this guide.

Concepted & Written by Rob Bedeaux
Designed by Dawn Fifer & Morgan Ramthun
Production art by Cali Schimberg & Keaton McAuliffe

ISBN 978-1-63944-371-0

Contents

1 Overview of the Olympic Games

2 Tokyo 2020 Olympic Sports

4 Answer Guide

5 Photo Credits

Overview OF THE OLYMPIC GAMES

Ancient Games

The origin of the ancient Olympic Games is lost in history, but some say that it began as a commemoration of the god Zeus' defeating Cronusin a wrestling match—the prize being possession of Earth. Other legends state that Heracles, son of Zeus and the mortal woman Alcmene, founded the Games. Regardless of the event that inspired the Games, the first recorded mention of the Olympics was in 776 BCE. The Olympic Games would continue to be held in Olympia in the western Peloponnese until 393 ACE.

While nominally a religious festival honoring the gods, a major part was the competition between young men who wanted to show off their physical fitness, strength, speed, and cunning. For five days, spectators would watch athletes compete in running, jumping, and throwing events plus boxing, wrestling, pankration, and chariot racing. Winners were awarded a crown of olive leaves, also known as kotinos. The olive branch and leaves were intertwined to form a circle or a horse-shoe and placed on the victor's head.

At its height in the second century ACE, 40,000 spectators would pack the stadium while many more lingered outside enjoying the festivities. In 393 ACE, Emperor Theodosius I, a Christian, banned all pagan festivals, ending the Olympic tradition after nearly 12 centuries.

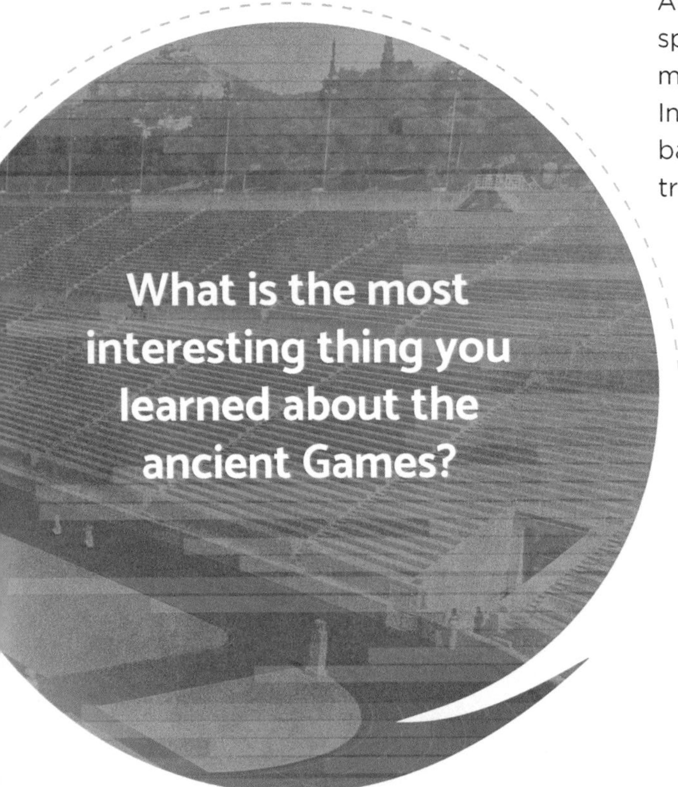

Learn More

To learn more about the ancient games scan the QR code above.

The Original Sports

An Olympiad begins with the holding of an Olympic Games and it last four years.

BOXING

CHARIOT RACING

DISCUS, JAVELIN, LONG JUMP

PANKRATION

RUNNING

WRESTLING

Question & Answer

1. When did the first Games take place?

____

2. Who was allowed to compete in these Games?

____

3. What did each winner receive as their prize?

____

4. For how many years did the Games originally last?

____

Athens

Olympia

It is 5,922 miles from Athens to Tokyo.

Fun Facts

1

A false start in track was grounds for corporal punishment (floggings).

2

There were only two rules in pankration—no biting and no gouging.

3

Athletes in combat sports had to indicate their surrender by raising their index fingers— some died before they could do this.

4

There were no points, no time limits, and no weight classifications in boxing.

Modern Games

In 1859, an Olympic-like event was first held in a square in Athens, then again in 1870 and 1875, with attendance topping 30,000 in 1870. However, these first events were all one-offs.

In 1892, Pierre de Coubertin, a French educator and historian, proposed a regularly recurring Olympic event. His idea took hold and in 1894, the first meeting of the International Olympic Committee (IOC) was held in Sorbonne, Paris. They agreed on an internationally rotating Olympic Games that would occur every four years.

In 1896, 14 countries competed in 43 different events in the first modern Olympic Games. As a tribute to the original games, it was held in Athens, Greece. The result was a big success. Athletes, fans and government officials were extremely enthusiastic about the future of the Games.

Unfortunately, the 1900 and 1904 World's Fairs relegated the Games to more of a sideshow at those events, instead of the grand international event that de Coubertin had envisioned. The Games regained their footing in 1908 and continued the four-year cycle known as an Olympiad until World War I, when the 1916 Games, which were to be held in Berlin, were canceled. This happened again in 1940 and 1944 because of World War II. The Games have run on schedule ever since until 2020, when the COVID-19 pandemic pushed the Games out of cycle to be held in July and August 2021.

Over the last 125 years, the Games have continued to grow and evolve. The Tokyo Olympics will feature 41 different sports, including newcomers like surfing, sport climbing, and skateboarding. Athletes from 206 nations are expected to compete. Women will also represent nearly fifty percent of the athletes, and they promise to be the most sustainable Games to date.

Where is the International Olympic Committee (IOC) based today?

Pierre de Coubertin

When Pierre de Coubertin was a young man, a German team of archaeologists were excavating ancient Olympia in Greece. De Coubertin was keenly interested in the discoveries and has repeatedly stated that this dig was the inspiration for recreating the ancient Games. Like the ancient Greeks, he saw sport as a spiritual movement and wanted to rebuild that for the modern day.

"Like ancient athletics, modern athletics is a religion, a belief, a passionate movement of the spirit that can range from 'games to heroism.'"

- Pierre de Couberti

Fill in the Blank

1. The first meeting of the International Olympic Committee (IOC) was held in ____________ (city, country) in ______ (year).

2. Women were officially allowed to compete starting in the ______ (year) Olympic Games.

3. The first modern Olympic Games was held in ____________ (city, country) in ______ (year).

Scan the QR code to learn more about the modern games.

Compare and Contrast the Ancient and Modern Games

In the Venn diagram, compare and contrast the Ancient and Modern Olympic Games. Where the circles overlap list common characteristics of both. On either side, list unique asoects of each.

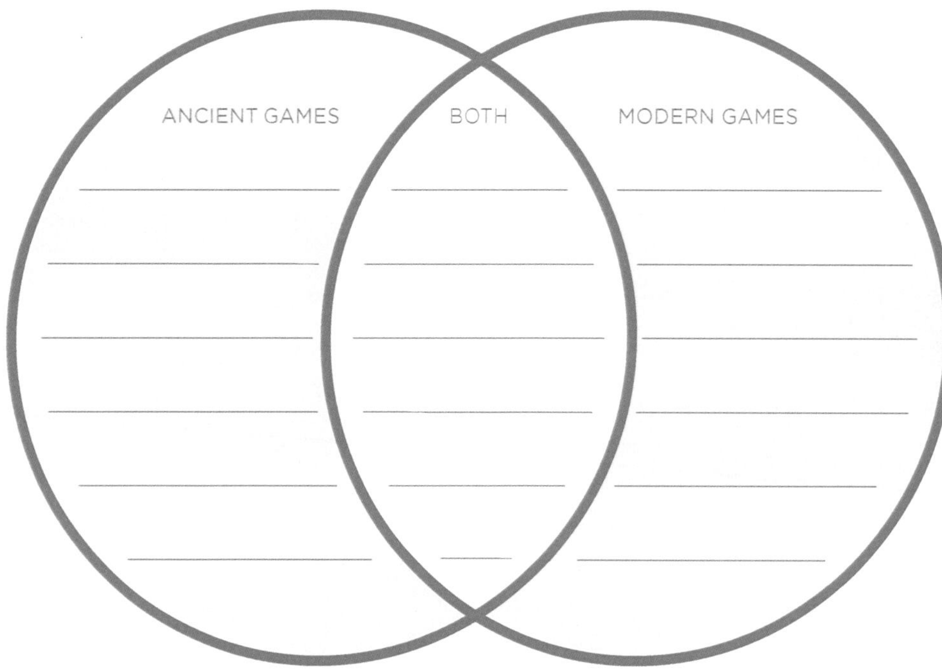

Fun Facts

1. Great Britain is the only nation to have won at least one gold medal at every Olympic Games.

2. Women have competed in the modern Olympics nearly as long as the Games have been around. In 1900, there were female athletes in sailing, tennis, croquet, equestrian, and golf.

3. 2021 marks the first time that the Olympics will be held in an odd-numbered year.

The Olympic Rings

The Olympic Rings are a relatively modern addition to the Games. They first appeared in 1913 at the top of a letter written by Baron Pierre de Coubertin, the founder of the modern Olympic Games. In the letter he wrote, "These five rings represent the five parts of the world now won over to the cause of Olympism and ready to accept its fertile rivalries. Moreover, the six colors thus combined reproduce those of all the nations without exception."

An often cited mistake is that each ring color represents individual content. Rather, the five colors combined with the white background represent the colors of the flags of all nations at that time, without exception.

The rings are interlaced to show the meeting of the athletes of the world during each edition of the Olympic Games in a spirit of good friendship and fair and equal competition.

Olympic Rings Tattoos

Freestyle swimmer Chris Jacobs is credited with starting the Olympic rings tradition. He noticed a small maple leaf tattoo on Canadian competitor Victor Davis' chest and decided to follow suit and celebrate his three gold medals by tattooing the rings just below the waistline of his swim trunks. A few years later he got a second set of rings tattooed on his bicep. It wasn't until 2008 when Michael Phelps got his tattoo that the tradition really took off. Today, it is a right of passage with many Olympians getting rings tattoos somewhere on their bodies.

Learn More

To learn more about the Olympic Rings scan the QR code above.

Compare & Contrast

What differences do you see in each version of the rings. Why do you suppose such minor changes were made?

1913

Introduced in 1913

1920

The rings were first used during the Games of the VII Olympiad in Antwerp 1920

1957

In 1957, the IOC approved a standardized version of the rings which varied only slightly from the original design proposed by Coubertin

1986

In 1986, the official representation of the rings was updated slightly to include spacing between each ring

2010

In 2010, the IOC approved a return to the interlocking ring design used prior to 1986

The Olympic Torch & Flame

Today the lighting of the Olympic flame is an integral part of the Games and provides a connection to its ancient history. However, it didn't make its first appearance until 32 years after the first modern Olympic Games. In these first appearances, the flame was lit over the stadium with much less fanfare than today.

Prior to the 1936 Games in Berlin, a German university lecturer, sports enthusiast, and head of Berlin's Olympic Organizing Committee proposed a grand torch relay from Olympia to the site of the current Games. The torch would then be used to light the Olympic flame and open the Games.

Rule 13 of the Olympic Charter states "The Olympic flame is the flame which is kindled in Olympia under the authority of the IOC" and must begin its journey in Olympia, Greece.

Learn More

To learn more about the Olympic torch and flame scan the QR code above.

Lighting of the Torch for Tokyo

The ceremony took place on March 12, 2020, at Olympia, Greece. However, due to the COVID-19 pandemic, the 31-city tour of Greece was canceled. A small ceremony was held in Sparta where Scottish actor Gerard Butler—who played Leonidas in the movie 300—helped commemorate the 2,500th anniversary of the Battle of Thermopylae.

The torch was later placed in the Japan Olympic Museum until the relay was restarted on March 25, 2021. It then made a tour of Japan and then on July 23, 2021 after a delay of one year, the cauldron will be lit to open the Tokyo 2020 Olympic Games.

Did You Know?

- A new torch is designed for every Olympics.
- Several torches are made because each torchbearer is given their own torch. The flame is passed from runner to runner, not the torch.
- As it was in Ancient Greece, the Mother Flame that is used to light the torch is lit by the sun in Olympia.
- Since 1928, a flame has been lit in the opening ceremony and remains lit until the closing ceremony.

DRAW TORCH HERE

The Olympic Torch relay is 121 days long

Past Olympic Torches

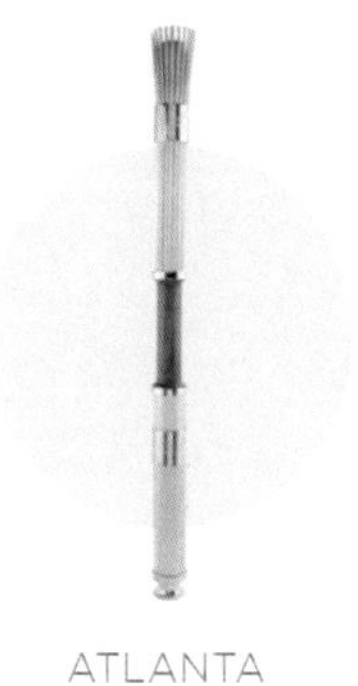
ATLANTA 1996

SYDNEY 2000

ATHENS 2004

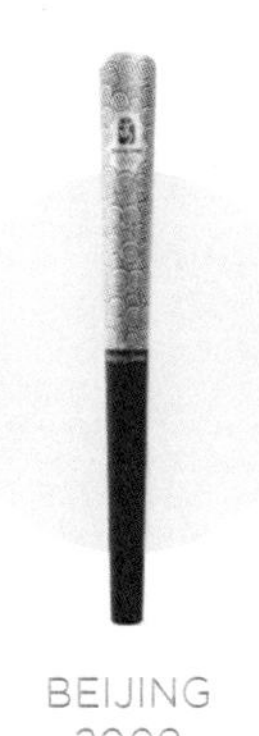
BEIJING 2008

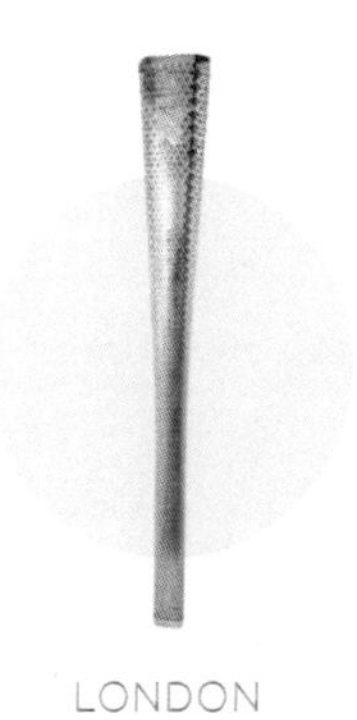
LONDON 2012

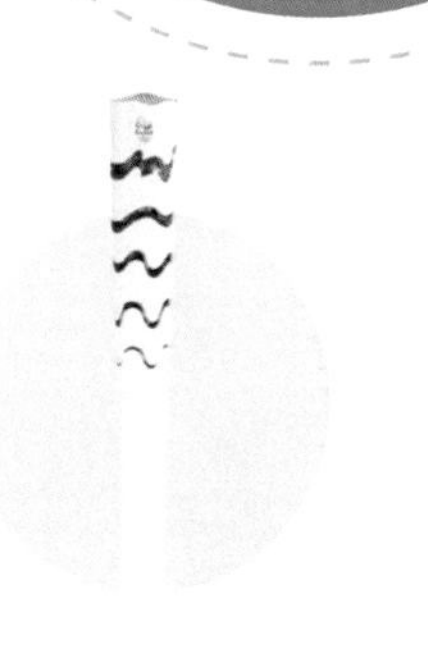
RIO DE JANEIRO 2016

Medals

Carrying on the tradition from the ancient Olympic Games, the first modern Games crowned the winners with an olive wreath and 1st & 2nd place winners received silver and bronze medals respectively. While the games in 1900, no medals were awarded at all. Finally, in 1904 winners received the traditional gold, silver, and bronze medals for 1st, 2nd, and 3rd place.

Some consistency emerged in 1928, when Italian artist Giuseppe Cassioli designed the medals for the Olympic Games in Amsterdam. Cassioli's design had several features: a robed Hellenic goddess holding a laurel wreath with the Athens Colosseum in the background, a horse drawn chariot, a Grecian urn, and the Olympic rings. They appeared on both sides of the medals until 1968. In 1972, the image started to be used only on the front side only.

In 2004, the IOC approved an updated version of this design.

2020 Tokyo Gold Medal

Scan to learn more about the medals.

Example Medals

ATHENS 1896

LONDON 1948

TOKYO 1964

LOS ANGELES 1984

SYDNEY 2000

RIO 2016

Design Your Own Medal

DRAW MEDAL FRONT HERE

DRAW MEDAL BACK HERE

The 2008 Beijing medals also included Jade.

Fun Facts

1

No Olympian has received a solid gold medal since the 1912 Games.

2

Gold medals are generally heavier than silver or bronze medals. For example, the Tokyo medals weigh 556g, 550g, and 450g, respectively.

3

Olympians are often seen biting their medals. This harkens back to the ancient practice of biting into gold to test its purity and authenticity.

4

It wasn't until 1960 that medals were designed to be worn around the neck. Prior to that, they were pinned to the winner's chest.

The Mascot

The Olympic and Paralympic mascots are fictional characters—usually an animal native to the area or human figures—who represent the cultural heritage of the place where the Olympic and Paralympic Games are taking place.

The first Olympic mascot was born at the Grenoble Olympic Games in 1968. It was named "Schuss" and was a little man on skis, designed in an abstract form and painted the colors of France (blue, red, and white). Starting in 1968, the coherent design system was introduced for the XIX Olympiad in Mexico. Building on the graphical success, 1972 Olympics in Munich introduced Waldi, a Dachshund dog, which was a popular breed in Bavaria and represented the attributes required for athletes—resistance, tenacity, and agility. It contained three of the colors of the Olympic flag (blue, yellow, green). From 1972 to date, every Olympics has featured a mascot the represents the feel of the Games and something of the host city.

The success of those first mascots helped the idea of a mascot become a symbol of the Olympic Games and developed into an institution.

Miraitowa

The 2020 Olympic mascot is called Miraitowa, which is derived from the Japanese words mirai (future) and towa (eternity). This name was chosen to promote a future full of eternal hope in the hearts of people all over the world.

Mascot Matching

Match the Tokyo Mascots to their sport.

CYCLING

EQUESTRIAN

HANDBALL

JUDO

SURFING

WEIGHTLIFTING

Draw Your Own Mascot

Question & Answer

What is your favorite mascot? Why?

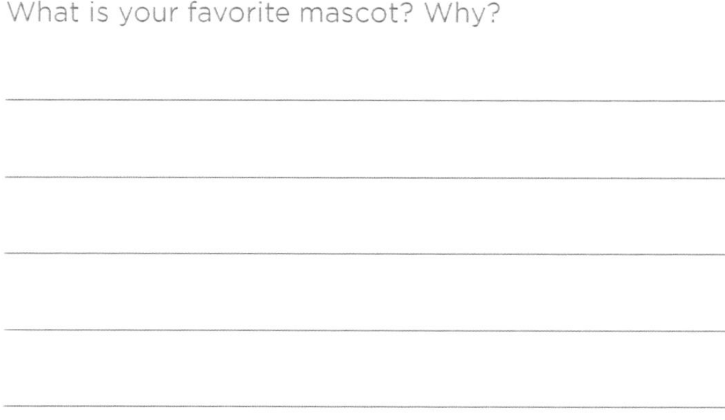

Scan the QR code to learn more about Olympic mascots.

DRAW MASCOT HERE

Schuss, Grenoble Olympic Games 1968

Mascot Timeline for the Olympic Games

MUNICH
1972

SEOUL
1988

BARCELONA
1992

ATLANTA
1996

LONDON
2012

RIO DE JANEIRO
2016

Sports

There are 41 sports represented at the Tokyo Olympics. This includes six new sports added since the 2016 Rio Games—baseball, softball, karate, sport climbing, skateboarding, and surfing.

Competing Countries

Did you know there are more independent entities competing in the Tokyo Olympics but only 195 different countries? That means that some countries have different contingents competing independent of one another. One of those is the United States! In addition to athletes competing under the stars and stripes, American Samoa, Guam, Puerto Rico, and the US Virgin Islands each have their own delegation at the games.

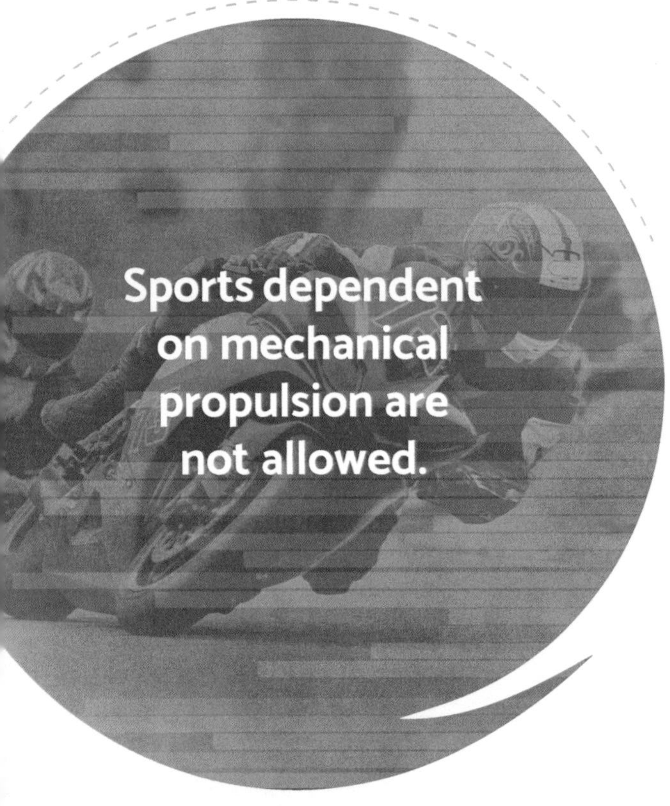

Scan me to learn more about Olympic sports.

American Samoa

Guam

Puerto Rico

US Virgin Islands

SWIMMING

DIVING

WATER POLO

MARATHON SWIMMING

ARTISTIC SWIMMING

Aquatics

Under the International Olympic Committee (IOC), swimming, diving, water polo, marathon swimming, and artistic swimming are all part of the same sport? They are all separate disciplines in the sport of aquatics. However, the U.S. treats each of these as its own sport with its own rules and governing body. It's only at the Olympic Games and other international competitions that they are combined under a single sport.

Olympic Sport Name Word Scramble

1 RCRAYHE ____________________

2 BEHAC LLOYLELAVB ____________________

3 MNNTAIBDO ____________________

4 EASLBBLA ____________________

5 ESTBKALLBA ____________________

6 XGOBNI ____________________

7 AOCNEGNI ____________________

8 IGYCLNC ____________________

9 DVGINI ____________________

10 UNQTASEIER ____________________

11 LEFDI HCYOEK ____________________

12 CNEIGFN ____________________

13 FOLG ____________________

14 YSAMCSIGNT ____________________

15 HNLDBAAL ____________________

16 OJDU ____________________

17 KREATA ____________________

18 DNOMRE ANTPTENOHL ____________________

19 WGORNI ____________________

20 BGURY ____________________

21 SAGILNI ____________________

22 IHNSGTOO ____________________

23 TAKANISODBEGR ____________________

24 ECRCOS ____________________

25 LASFBTOL ____________________

26 PRSOT MCNLBGII ____________________

27 GSRFNUI ____________________

28 NWGMIMSI ____________________

29 LTEAB INETSN ____________________

30 WODTAEOKN ____________________

Tug-o-war used to be an Olympic sport

31 SNITEN ____________________

32 KTRAC NDA LFDIE ____________________

33 RMNTIOEALP ____________________

34 ORNTHLTIA ____________________

35 VALOLLELYB ____________________

36 ARWET OPLO ____________________

37 HILGGITNTFEWI ____________________

38 SGLIRTWEN ____________________

Opening Ceremony

The Opening Ceremony has been part of the Olympic Games since its modern inception in 1896. While many parts have changed, some of the traditions from that first Games have carried on to today. The Olympic anthem composed for the 1896 Games is still played and the parade of athletes entering the stadium (called the Parade of Nations) is considered the highlight for most spectators.

Today, Rule 55 of the Olympic Charter governs much of the protocol, but each host country provides its own flavor, especially to the artistic part of the program. Each Opening Ceremony concludes with the lighting of the Olympic flame, signaling the official beginning of the Games.

Scan the QR code to learn more about the Opening Ceremony.

Watch All of the Action

NBC will air its first-ever live morning broadcast of an Olympic Opening Ceremony from Tokyo as part of its daylong presentation on Friday, July 23, 2021.

EASTERN TIME

6:55 AM	- 11:00 AM	Live Opening Ceremony Coverage
11:00 AM	- 1:00 PM	Special Edition of TODAY
1:00 PM	- 4:00 PM	Tokyo Olympics Daytime
7:30 PM	- 12:00 AM	Primetime Opening Ceremony
12:35 AM	- 5:00 AM	Overnight Replay of Opening Ceremony

The Elements

While watching the Opening Ceremony, make note of each of the activities below and put them in the proper order that you see them.

_______ The opening of the Games

_______ Raising the Olympic flag & playing the anthem

_______ The artistic program

_______ The symbolic release of doves

_______ Official speeches

_______ Olympic Laurel

_______ Playing the National Anthem

_______ Taking of the Olympic oath

_______ Olympic flame and torch relay

_______ Parade of Nations *(also known "Parade of Athletes")*

_______ Entry into the stadium and welcome

Observations

1. Describe the Olympic flag. ______________________________

____

2. How many countries are competing at the Tokyo 2020 Olympics? ______________________________

3. How many sports are in the Tokyo Olympic Games? ______________________________

4. What are some interesting facts that you learned about Japan? ______________________________

____

____

____

Olympic champion Michael Phelps carrying the United States flag while leading the Olympic team USA in the Rio 2016 Opening Ceremony at Maracana Stadium

What was your favorite part of the Opening Ceremony?

Closing Ceremony

The Closing Ceremony marks the end of the Games and has been part of the modern games since its inception in 1896. However, the Parade of Athletes didn't come into existence until 1956. It is one final chance for the athletes to come together and celebrate as 'one nation' and reaffirm the Olympic spirit and values of Citius—Altius—Fortius (or Faster)—Higher—Stronger.

2016 Rio De Janeiro Closing Ceremony

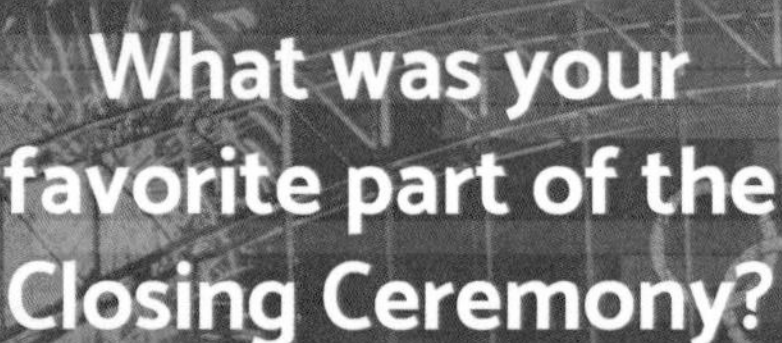

Learn More

To learn more about the Closing Ceremony scan the QR code above.

The Elements

While watching the Closing Ceremony, make note of each of the activities below and put them in the proper order that you see them.

_______ Parade of Athletes

_______ Moment of Remembrance

_______ Playing the National Anthem

_______ OCOG president's speech & IOC president's speech

_______ Entry of the nation's flags

_______ Extinguishing the Olympic Flame

_______ Intro of the Athletes' Commissions new members

_______ Next host city artistic segment

_______ Victory ceremony

_______ Lowering the Olympic flag & flag handover ceremon

_______ Playing of the Greek National anthem

_______ Entry and welcome

Observations

1. What made the Closing Ceremony unique?

____

____

2. What medals were awarded during the Closing Ceremony?

____

____

3. Who carried the flag after it was lowered and to whom was it given?

____

____

4. What is the next host city for the Olympic Games in 2024?

____

Mayor Eduardo Paes of Rio de Janeiro, IOC President Thomas Bach, and Governor Yuriko Koike of Tokyo take part in the Flag Handover Ceremony during the Rio 2016 Olympic Games at Maracana Stadium

Tokyo
2020 OLYMPIC SPORTS

Archery

Archery is a popular competitive and recreational sport that requires intense focus and precision. Archers use a bow to shoot arrows at targets of varying distances, hoping to hit the center.

How the Sport Began

Archery is one of the oldest sports still practiced today. It can be traced back to France, 15,000 years ago! The modern history of target archery goes back to the 1300s, when the longbow became the most important weapon in the English army. Even after archery fell out of use in the military, people of all classes continued to enjoy it for recreational purposes.

Track the Medals

Understanding the Sport

In the Olympics, archers shoot at targets that are four feet in diameter. Each target is divided into five colored rings. A 'bullseye' or 'pinhole' requires hitting a circle only 4.8 inches in diameter.

During the first round, the target is set 230 feet from the archer, and they shoot 72 arrows and receive up to ten points per arrow (a perfect score is 720 points). Athletes then compete in a head-to-head bracket-style format similar to tennis.

The Tokyo Olympics will have five events (including a new mixed gender team event). The ranking round determines the order, or seed, that archers receive for the main competition. Each pair of archers will shoot up to three arrows from 70 feet per set, with a maximum of 5 ends. The first competitor to reach 6 set points wins and advances to the next round.

Trenton Cowles

Tokyo Olympic Hopeful

A fan of the Wii's archery video game, Cowles decided to take it into the the real world. He made a bow out a bungee & a stick and started taking shots in his back yard. That led him to Gold at the 2018 Buenos Aires Youth Olympic Games.

ARCHERY BROADCAST SCHEDULE

Medal Match

7/24 7/25 7/26 7/30 7/31

Watch all of the action on the networks of NBCUniversal including

Who's Competing?

Follow your favorite athletes.

NAME	SCORE

Scan me for more!

Did You Know?

Only a recurve bow is used in the Olympics. The bow is named for its distinct shape; central parts curving toward the archer, and the tips curving away. This design provides more power but needs less strength to use.

Fun Facts

A royal decree in 1363 required all English gentlemen to practice archery on Sundays and holidays.

Paleontologists believe the use of bows and arrows for hunting developed as early as 35,000 BCE!

South Korea is the most decorated country with 39 total medals including 23 gold, nine silver, and seven bronze medals.

Word Scramble

MAR RDGUA ______________________

CRLEIKC ______________________

EGCLNHTIF ______________________

IBLM ______________________

KNOC ______________________

VQUEIR ______________________

SIERR ______________________

RONBI ODHO ______________________

FAHTS ______________________

IABIZSLRTE ______________________

Compare & Contrast

3D archery is another popular type of archery. It differs from Olympic archery in that, it simulates the hunting experience. The targets are designed to look like animals and the archer walks the course looking for targets. How is this different from Olympic archery?

Archery

Target Maze

Discussion Questions

1. With the invention of firearms (guns), the use of the bow and arrow declined. Why do you think that is?

2. Notice the different size circles and colors on the target. What do you think they are used for?

3. Many types of arrows included feathers (fletching) at the end of them. What do you suppose those are for?

Want to know more about Archery?
Visit USA Archery at www.usarchery.org

Artistic Swimming

Considered "ornamental" or "scientific" swimming, there a series of core moves that swimmers must complete. Competitors are required to stay in sync with music played above and below the waterline. Scoring is based on synchronization, difficulty and choreography.

How the Sport Began

Artistic swimming developed around the turn of the 20th Century, with the first competitions being held in Berlin and England (both were men only). Eventually, the sport was considered better suited for women because they were more buoyant and able to create better images in the water.In the early 20th century traveling water shows and hollywood helped popularize the sport.

Track the Medals

Understanding the Sport

In the duet competition, a preliminary free routine of up to three minutes is performed. The next day duets perform a technical routine of up to 2 minutes 20 seconds. The pairs must perform the required elements in sequence throughout the routine, with an emphasis on execution.

The team competition comprises groups of eight athletes per country. Each team first performs a technical routine of up to 2 minutes 50 seconds, where athletes must execute seven required elements in sequence. The next day they perform a 4 minute freestyle routine.

In both formats, the scores are combined to construct the final ranking

Scan me for more!

Mother of Artistic Swimming

She helped push the sport forward in 1915 when she added music to the routines. Eventually, the strokes were synced up with the beats in the music, as in dancing.

Who's Competing?

Follow your favorite athletes.

NAME	POSITION

ARTISTIC SWIMMING BROADCAST SCHEDULE

Duet	Team
8/4	8/7

Watch all of the action on the networks of NBCUniversal including

Did You Know?

The movie Neptunes Daughter is about Annette Kellerman who performed in a glass tank and is described as the worlds first under-water ballerina.

Fun Facts

The nose clip is an essential. It allows swimmers to perform leg movements and elements upside-down without getting water in their nose.

Only the USA, Canada, Japan, Russia, China, Spain, and France have medaled in this sport.

The US had won a medal in every event in Olympic history before 2000. It has not won a medal since 2004.

Discussion Questions

1. In both team and duet routines, there are a required set of figures that need to be done. Why do you suppose everyone has to perform the same moves?

Artistic Swimming

Crossword

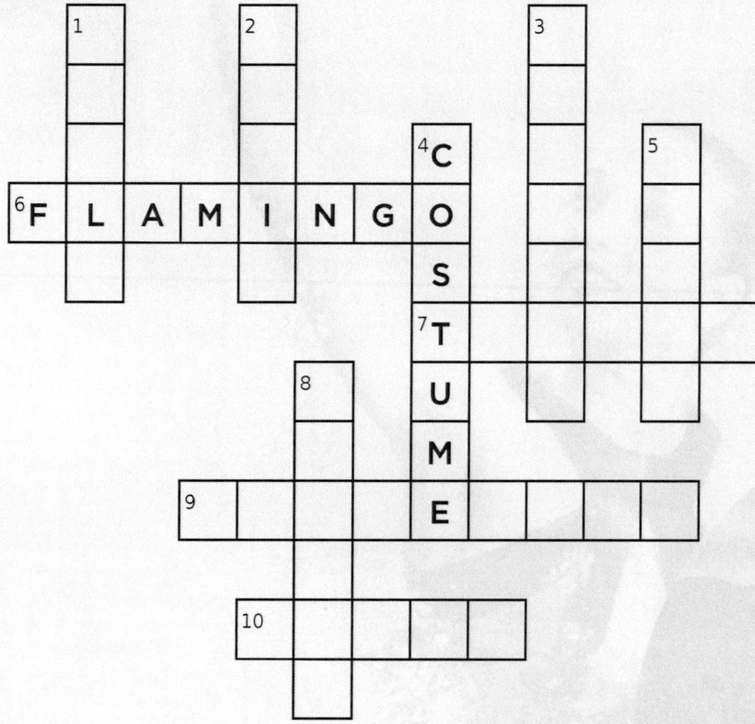

DOWN

1 A movement of the hands designed to apply continuous pressure against the water to propel, balance, and support the body while treading water.

2 A position where the legs are split evenly forward and back, with the feet and thighs at the surface while the lower back is arched and the hips, shoulders, and head are in a vertical line with the water.

3 A formation made by the spatial relationship between the members of a team.

4 Typically dress in brightly colored swim suits with matching or coordinated head/ hair pieces and dramatic, waterproof stage makeup.

5 A quick head-first rise out of the water; the aim is to raise as much of the body above the surface as possible.

8 A combination of body positions and transitions performed in a prescribed manner.

ACROSS

6 A position where one leg is extended perpendicular to the surface of the water while the other leg is drawn to the chest, with the lower leg parallel to the surface and the face at the surface.

7 A move that starts from a back pike position with the legs perpendicular to the surface and involves a rapid vertical upward movement of the legs and hips as the body unrolls to assume the vertical position.

9 A rotary action of the legs used to support and propel the upper body in an upright position, leaving the arms free.

10 A position where the body is extended in a vertical position with one leg extended forward at a 90 degree angle.

Want to know more about Artistic Swimming?
Visit USA Artistic Swimming at www.teamusa.org/usa-artistic-swimming

Badminton

Badminton is the second-most popular participation sport in the world behind soccer (football). Similar to tennis, it's a court or lawn game played with lightweight rackets and a shuttlecock.

While elite players can run up to four miles around the court during a match, its casual play and simple rules make it a great game for any age or skill level.

How the Sport Began

It's up for debate as to whether badminton came from the Aztecs in Mexico or from a game in India called Poona. Either way, it received its name in 1870 from English officers who constructed a shuttlecock out of a champagne cork and chicken feathers. They dubbed the game badminton after the Badminton Estate.

Seven years later, a colonel published the official rules and in 1934, the International Badminton Federation (IBF) was founded by nine members — the United States was not included. Badminton finally became an Olympic sport in 1992. China has won 41 medals, making them the most decorated country.

Understanding the Sport

Badminton is played with racquets and a feathered shuttle (or shuttlecock). Opposing players, or teams of two, face off over a 5-foot 1-inch net and attempt to win a best-of-three set of games.

Each "game" is played to 21 points; 1 point is awarded to whichever side wins the volley. One side must win by 2 points. If the score is 'tied' at 29 points, the winner of the next point wins.

Badminton at the Olympics is made up of 5 events: men's and women's singles, men's and women's doubles, and mixed doubles. Athletes qualify based on the Badminton World Federation's ranking list.

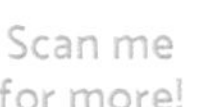

Track the Medals

Lin Dan

Two Time Olympic Champion

Widely regarded as the greatest badminton player of all time. Lin has completed the "Super Grand Slam" which is the winner of the 9 major badminton titles.

BADMINTON BROADCAST SCHEDULE

Medal Match

7/30 7/31 8/1 8/2

Watch all of the action on the networks of NBCUniversal including

Fun Facts

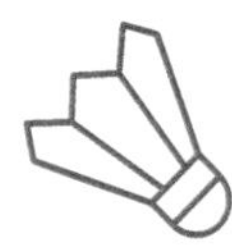

Olympic-caliber players can hit the shuttle at speeds of up to 200 mph, which has resulted in lost teeth and broken glasses!

The longest badminton match on record lasted for two hours, 41 minutes. The shortest match lasted only six minutes!

The Kansas City Art Museum's lawn is home to the world's largest shuttlecocks. The four decorative shuttlecocks are 19 feet tall and weigh nearly three tons.

Did You Know?

Shuttles have 16 feathers and usually last for no more than two games.

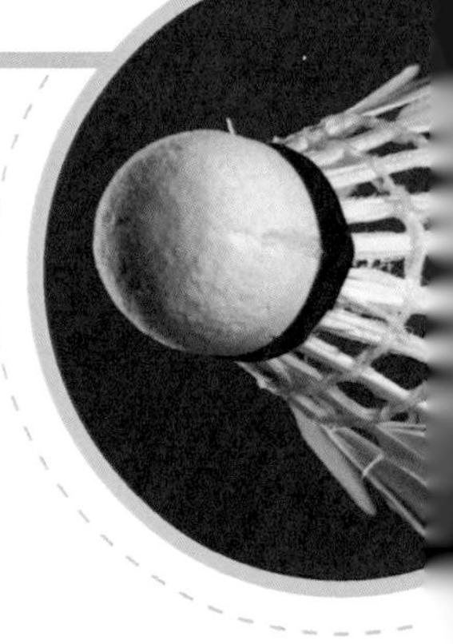

Badminton

Word Search

```
T M B Y W R P L H P X F I J D
P E Z J P Z L F K R Q L T A U
B X W J L H X E R F S I B H O
I R E Q G C R X T W M C A B U
L W K F C K A Z W X A K C W F
D Y Y B M R M Y G B S E K N A
E T I X L D O E R Z H N C S U
X C Y K E V H S X D T P O L L
N D V R A T O A S F V B U Z T
E Q D S H X D X U C E D R I W
Z Z Z C A R R Y P D O Z T Z P
I B U P S E P G U H F U F W C
X S H U T T L E C O C K R Y F
T L R K R A L L Y Z D V R T H
B E T J I M L Z U A H R F C N
```

BACKCOURT
CARRY
CROSS-COURT
FAULT
FLICK
LET
RALLY
SHUTTLECOCK
SMASH

Compare & Contrast

Compare and contrast the advantages and disadvantages of singles, doubles, and mixed events.

____

____

Discussion Questions

1. Players serve from the right side if their score is an even number and the left side if their score is an odd number. Why do you think that is?

2. Why do you suppose the shuttlecock has feathers on it?

Name the Elements

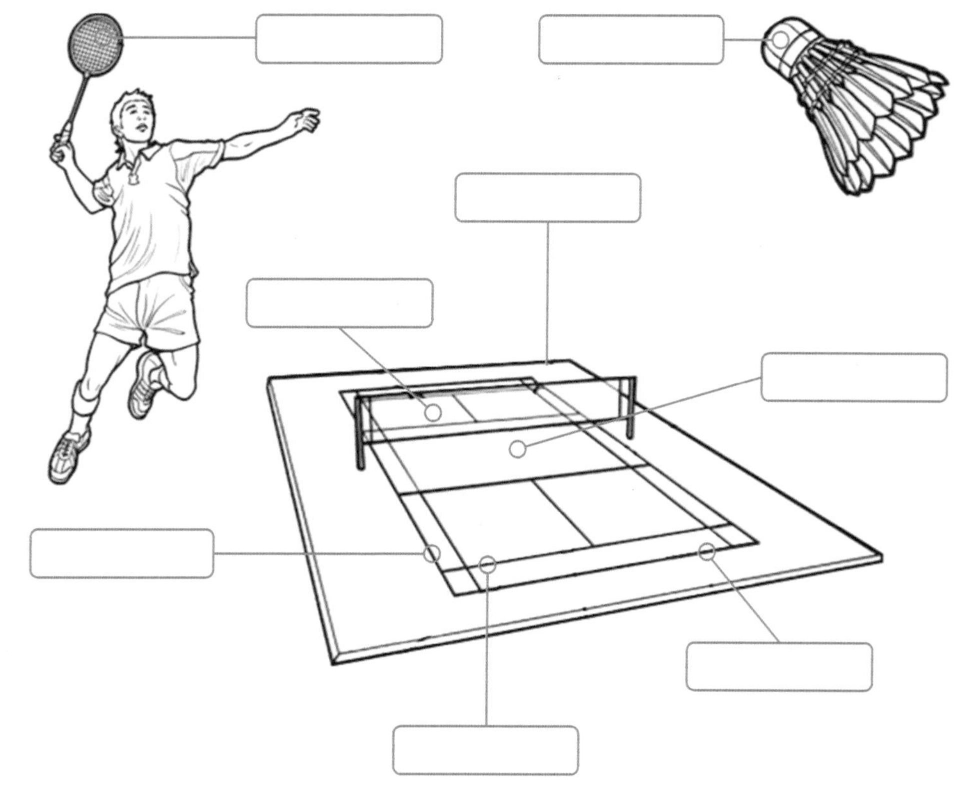

Baseball

Baseball is a game played with a bat, a ball, and a glove. The fundamentals of the game involve throwing, hitting, and catching the ball. Unlike most games, a running clock does not limit the length of a game. Two competing teams play over a period of innings, which are divided into halves. Professional and college games are generally nine innings.

How the Sport Began

Baseball evolved from older bat-and-ball games already being played in the mid-18th century. This game was brought by immigrants to North America, where the modern version developed.

By the late 19th century, baseball was widely recognized as the national sport of the United States. Baseball is popular in North America and parts of Central and South America, the Caribbean, and East Asia, particularly in Japan, South Korea, and Chinese Taipei (Taiwan).

Understanding the Sport

The competition will be limited to just six teams including Japan, who as the host city receives a spot. The teams are split into two groups for an initial round and then a complex knockout round follows.

Rules are nearly identical with Major League Baseball. Exceptions include a mercy rule where if a team is leading by 10 or more runs after 7 innings, they win, and an extra innings rule where if competition is tied at the 10th inning, base runners are automatically placed on first and second base with no outs.

Pedro Luis Lazo Iglesias

Track the Medals

Two Time Olympic Champion

Part of Team Cuba, this pitcher led his team to gold in 1996 & 2004 and claimed silver in 2000 & 2008. During the '96 Olympics, his team won all 18 games played!

BASEBALL BROADCAST SCHEDULE

Medal Games

8/7

Watch all of the action on the networks of NBCUniversal including

Fun Facts

The overhand pitch was introduced in 1886. Even today, there is no rule stating that a pitcher can't pitch underhand!!

The first World Series was played between Pittsburgh and Boston in 1903 —it was a best-of-nine-game series.

Second base is the most stolen base because it is the farthest from home plate and requires a longest throw.

Who's on the team?

Follow your favorite athletes.

NAME	POSITION

Scan me for more details about Baseball!

Did You Know?

The longest baseball game in MLB history lasted 26 innings.

Crossword

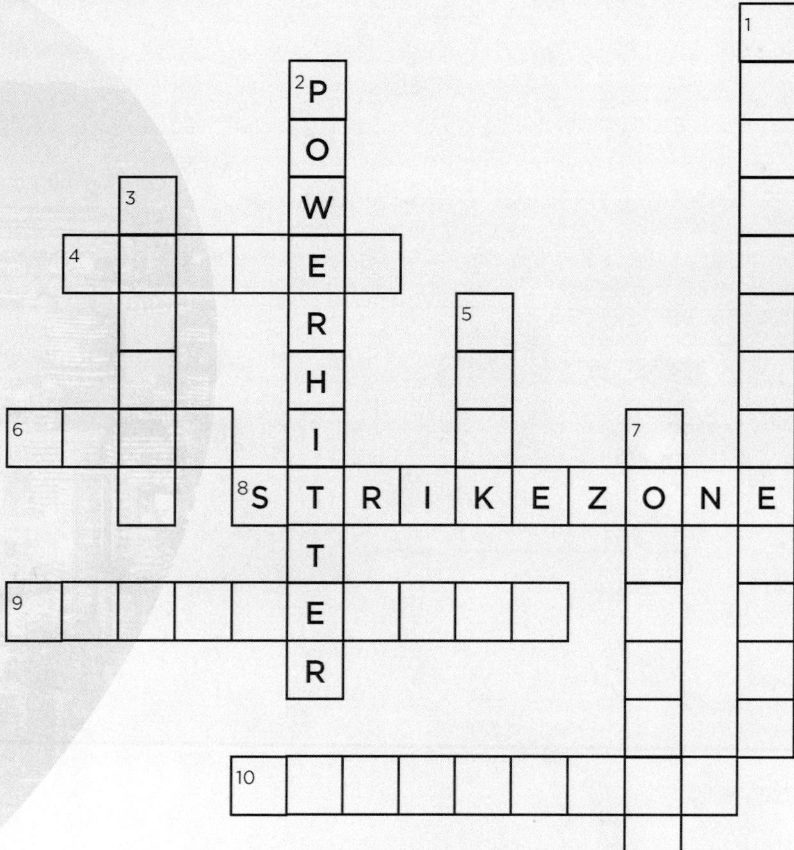

DOWN

1 After an out is recorded, teams throw the ball around the infield

2 A skilled batter that hits the baseball far, usually for home runs or extra bases

3 When a base runner is in a rundown

5 When the pitcher tries to trick the base runners with illegal motions

7 Third base position

ACROSS

4 Home Run

6 When the pitcher throws four balls to a batter, the batter gets to walk to first base

8 The area over home plate, above the batter's knees

9 A defensive play that results in two players being tagged out

10 When the pitch count has 3 balls and 2 strikes.

Baseball

Picture Math

Can you solve the equation?

(baseball) + (baseball) + (baseball) = 30

(bats) + (bats) + (baseball) = 14

(bats) + (glove) + (glove) = 8

(baseball) + (glove) + (bat) = __

Compare & Contrast

Describe the differences between a baseball and softball diamond.

____

____

Discussion Questions

1. Baseball has been absent from the Olympics since 2008, but Japan used their hosting status to bring it back. Why do you think that is?

Basketball

Basketball is one of the world's most popular sports. It's a game played between two teams of five players on a rectangular court, usually indoors. Each team tries to score by tossing the ball through the opponent's hoops.

While basketball is competitively a winter sport, it can be played all year long — on playgrounds, church halls, in school yards, family driveways, and in summer camps — often on an informal basis between two or more contestants.

How the Sport Began

Unlike most sports, basketball did not evolve from an older game. In 1891, a physical education class at a YMCA training college in Springfield, Massachusetts, was asked to come up with an indoor winter game that would be attractive to young men.

Canadian student James Naismith came up with a solution — he nailed peach baskets along the railing at each end of the gym and created rules, which included throwing a soccer ball through the peach baskets. The game quickly evolved into something that more closely resembles the modern-day version.

BASKETBALL BROADCAST SCHEDULE

Men	Women
8/7	8/8

Watch all of the action on the networks of NBCUniversal including

Understanding Olympic Basketball

Both 3x3 and 5x5 basketball will be contested in Tokyo While they come from the same roots, the two games differ drastically with 3x3 being a much faster game. Some of the significant rules differences include only using a ½ court, only 3 players per team on the court, a 12 second vs 24 second shot clock, and games end after one team scores 21 points or 10 minutes. Because of these and other rules, agility rather than endurance and offense rather than defense are keys to success.

Track the Medals

Sue Bird

Tokyo Olympic Hopeful

Bird has already won 4 Olympic Gold Medals! As a youth Bird diversified her skills by playing soccer & tennis and running track.

Scan for more information about Basketball!

Did You Know?

Michael Jordan's shoes used to be against the NBA's dress code, with the red and black color combination he called the "Devil's colors."

Fun Facts

The slam dunk was originally known as a dunk shot. Lakers announcer Chick Hearn coined the term "slam dunk."

The first basketball game was played with a soccer ball and peach baskets.

The three-pointer wasn't introduced until the 1979-80 NBA season.

Word Scramble

LAPYLEOO ______________________

ANKB TOHS ______________________

CENHB ______________________

RGIHNACG ______________________

UDEOBL IBLDRBE ______________________

URFULOTLC RSEPS ______________________

GHIH OSTP ______________________

COLINRKLDPA ______________________

XISTH MNA ______________________

RTEHENOTIP PAYL ______________________

Discussion Question

Why was the 1992 team called the "Dream Team"?

Compare & Contrast

3x3 basketball and 5x5 basketball both will be contested at the Tokyo Olympics. Compare and contrast the two types of basketball.

____

____

____

____

For help, watch www.sportsengine.com/basketball/3x3-versus-5x5-basketball

Basketball

Complete the Court

What makes up a basketball game? Fill this empty court with the complete basketball set-up, from court lines, players, etc.

- Court lines
- Baskets
- Coaching Staff
- Starters
- Referees
- Bench Players
- Audience

Beach Volleyball

Beach volleyball is played by two teams of two players. The ball can be hit with any part of the body, except while serving, which must be hit with the hand or the arm. The object is to send the ball over the net to ground it on the opponent's court, and to prevent the ball from being grounded on its own court. Each team has a maximum of three hits.

How the Sport Began

The sport began in Santa Monica in the early 1920s and arrived in Brazil in the 1930s.. It was known for its attitude and flair. By the 1980s, beach volleyball hit its stride. Sponsorships multiplied, offering prizes in excess of $20,000 for each event of the USA tour. Beach volleyball was the biggest growth sport from 1987 to 1994 increasing participation 38%. While the US has dominated gold at the Olympics, Brazil has more overall medals in the sport.

Track the Medals

Understanding the Sport

Beach volleyball consists of men's and women's doubles. Matches are best two-out-of-three sets. Rally scoring will be used – the team winning a rally scores a point, regardless of who serves. When the serving team wins a rally, it scores a point and continues to serve; when the returning team wins a rally, it scores a point and gains the right to serve.

In the first two sets, the first team to score 21 points wins the set. In the third set, the first team to score 15 points wins the set and the match.

April Ross

Tokyo Olympic Qualifier

Ross started playing at thirteen along with track. In 2006, she switched to beach volleyball and excelled, winning silver & bronze in 2012 and 2016, respectively. Is gold in the cards in Tokyo?

BEACH VOLLEYBALL BROADCAST SCHEDULE

Men	Women
8/7	8/6

Watch all of the action on the networks of NBCUniversal including

Fun Facts

Announced in Aug 2012, Misty May-Treanor is part of an elite group of athletes to appear on the iconic Wheaties box.

Beach volleyball is the only Olympic sport that has a rule prohibiting players from wearing too much!

Olympic powerhouses were those countries with 'beach culture.' However, at the 2004 Games Switzerland won a surprise bronze medal.

Who's on the team?

Follow your favorite athletes.

NAME	POSITION

Scan for more about Beach Volleyball!

Did You Know?

Teammates discuss strategy by using hand signals behind their back so to block the other team from seeing them.

Discussion Questions

1. A regulation beach volleyball is up to 1.5″ larger than an indoor volleyball. The court is also smaller than an indoor court. Why do you suppose these changes were made?

2. Beach volleyball doesn't have specific positions. Players hit, block, and dig. Why would every player need to know all these skills?

Compare & Contrast

Compare men's and women's uniforms in beach volleyball. How do they differ? If so why do you suppose that is?

____

____

____

Beach Volleyball

Crossword

DOWN

1 When an offensive player attacks the ball with a one-arm motion done over the head, attempting to get a kill.

2 An easy serve that flies high into the sky and over the net.

3 An attempt by a player or players to interrupt the ball before, as or just after it crosses the net.

5 Ball brought up, or saved, with any part of the body, particularly off a spike attempt.

7 An attempt to put the ball down on the opponent's side of the net for a kill, thus gaining a point or sideout.

ACROSS

4 Termination of a play leading to a point or side out.

6 An attempt by a player to conceal the start of a teammate's serve by obstructing an opponent's line of sight.

7 A served ball that lands within the playing boundaries.

8 A ball that is played close to the net with the hitter and blocker simultaneously contacting the ball.

9 An attack which is deflected off an opponent (usually during a block) and is unplayable resulting in a point for the attacking team.

Boxing

Boxing is a combat sport divided into two types — professional and amateur — in which two people, usually wearing protective gloves, throw punches at each other for a predetermined amount of time. Victory is achieved by the athlete who successfully lands more blows to their opponent's head and torso.

How the Sport Began

Boxing first emerged in present-day Ethiopia around 4000 B.C. The sport was formalized in 19th century Great Britain, with rules that included the wearing of gloves. Since then, boxers have become renowned for their sporting demeanor, with opponents showing immense respect for each other's courage and physical commitment. Boxing has appeared since the 1904 Olympic Games. Women's events were contested for the first time in 2012.

Understanding the Sport

Boxing is a combat sport in which two people throw punches at each other for a predetermined amount of time in a boxing ring.

Olympic boxing is overseen by a referee over a series of 3 rounds; each lasting 3 minutes. Five judges sit at the side of the ring and individually award points for successful hits.

The referee can end the match if they decide that the match should not continue or if a doctor indicates the match should be stopped. A match will also end if a competitor receives three warnings (penalties) and is disqualified, or if a competitor is unable to resume a fight within 10 seconds, considered knocked out ('KO').

Scan me for more!

Track the Medals

Chantel Navarro

LA28 Olympic Hopeful

16 year old Mexican-American Navarro has only been boxing since 2016, but already has eyes on Paris '24 and Los Angeles 2'8.

Who's Competing?

Follow your favorite athletes.

NAME	WINS/LOSSES

BOXING BROADCAST SCHEDULE

Men

8/3 8/4 8/5 8/6 8/7 8/8

Women

8/3 8/7 8/8

Watch all of the action on the networks of NBCUniversal including

Fun Facts

Announced in 1999 for Black History Month, this box commemorated three-time heavy weight champion, Muhammad Ali.

A boxing-type sport was part of the ancient Olympic Games around 688 BCE. and referenced in Homer's Iliad.

The youngest Olympic boxing medalist is Jackie Fields, who won gold at the 1924 Olympics at 16 years old.

Did You Know?

The first boxing gloves were known as "muffers," used to protect the hands and face.

Boxing

Word Search

K S H S K K U R B W C N R X P

F X Q N N C H T D D O K E A D

W W N G E R G P K R M G Z K I

A I T U U F Z Y T X B Z F N E

L Y Y D T K E S I I I M C O V

K Z Z C R H R I C T N X J C N

O R H Q A O L G N B A K F K A

V O D A L V T J W T T T O D J

E U W G C W W L X G I B O O T

R N L L O Z E T L S O L T W S

Q D P R R J Z A P Q N O W N N

V T S H N A Y I V R B W O O N

T Y L I E I S D Q I J S R D E

V S H H R X S U C J N U K S W

D N J Y Z V W R Z V K G B P P

BLOW	FOOTWORK	ROUND
COMBINATION	KNOCKDOWN	WALKOVER
FEINT	NEUTRAL CORNER	WEAVING

Compare & Contrast

Compare and contrast the advantages and disadvantages of each weight class.

Boxing Maze

Help the boxer reach his opponent.

Discussion Questions

1. Unlike in professional boxing matches, Olympic competitors wear a padded helmet. Why do you think that is?
2. Lighter weight classes have a different approach to boxing than heavier classes. What do you think those are?

Canoeing

Canoe sprint and canoe slalom are two disciplines that will be contested at the Olympic Games in Tokyo. Sprint athletes compete on a flatwater course in a canoe or a kayak while slalom athletes compete on a whitewater course and navigate upstream and downstream gates in a canoe or a kayak

How the Sport Began

The first recorded competitive canoe sprint race was organized by John MacGregor at the British Royal Canoe Club in 1869. The New York Canoe Club, founded in 1871, began North America's organization of the sport. In 1880, the American Canoe Association became the governing body in the United States. Canoe slalom began in Switzerland in 1933. Canoe sprint was added to the Olympics in 1936 and canoe slalom wasn't consistently added until 1992.

Track the Medals

CANOEING BROADCAST SCHEDULE

Slalom

7/26 7/27 7/29 7/30

Sprint

8/3 8/5 8/7

Watch all of the action on the networks of NBCUniversal including

Understanding the Sport

Canoe sprint athletes compete on a flatwater course in a canoe or a kayak. Athletes in each heat or round begin together at the start line and race to the finish line. In Tokyo, there will be 12 sprint events contested: six for men, six for women. The goal is to reach the finish line in the fastest time possible. Canoe slalom athletes compete on a whitewater course and navigate upstream and downstream gates in a canoe or a kayak. Unlike in canoe sprint, athletes go down the course one at a time and race against the clock. Competitors can be given time penalties for missing a gate or other mistakes.

Tokyo Olympic Qualifier

Only 19 years old, Nevin is one of two Americans to win a world canoe sprint title.

Who's Competing?

Follow your favorite athletes.

NAME	TIME

Scan for more information about Canoeing!

Fun Facts

When Jon Lugball, 5-time world champion appeared on a Wheaties box, canoeing was not an Olympic sport.

When referring to canoes and kayaks in the games, they are abbreviated with 'C' and 'K'.

The world's oldest boat is a canoe. Discovered in the Netherlands, it's believed to be around 10,000 years old.

Did You Know?

The Tokyo Games will be the first gender equal Games in history, meaning there will be the same number of male and female athletes.

Crossword

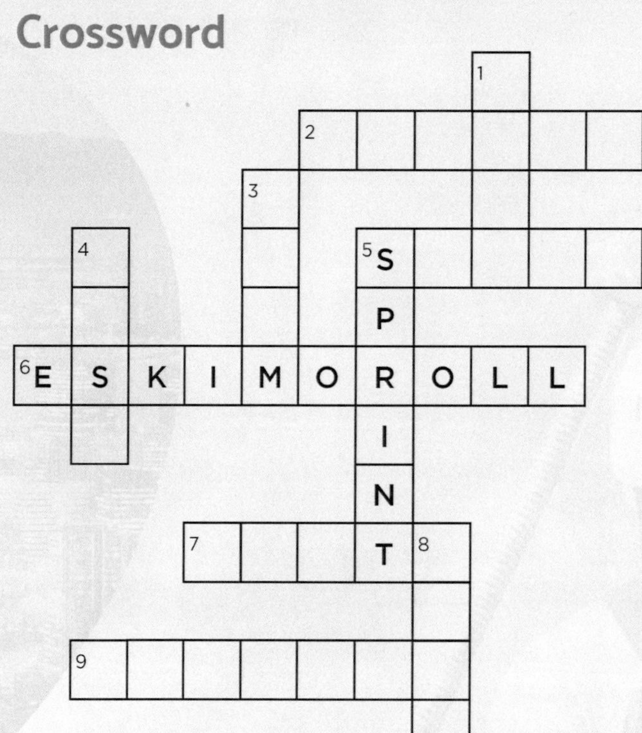

DOWN

1 Two striped poles hanging just above the water from a wire extending across the course.

3 The widest part of a canoe

4 The rough or broken water left behind a moving boat.

5 A straight canoe/kayak race on open, flat water

8 A pool of calmer water out of the main current of a stream

ACROSS

2 To become caught in the current against an obstruction and turn sideways

5 A stroke made in a broad curve, turning a canoe in the direction opposite the sweeping side when performed by the sternsman

6 When a boat capsizes, but the paddler remains in place as the boat "rolls" into an upright position

7 An area in which a whitewater course suddenly is constricted, compressing and amplifying the current's energy into a narrow tongue of water

9 A paddler who kneels or sits in the forward position of a canoe or kayak

Canoeing

Compare & Contrast

Name three differences between canoeing and kayaking at the Olympics.

Discussion Questions

1. Canoers only use a single bladed paddle, while kayakers have a double blade. What do you think are the advantages or disadvantages of each?

2. Look at the shape differences of the canoe and the kayak. Which do you think would be more challenging in slalom, or in sprint events?

3. Olympic slalom courses are almost always artificial. Why do you think that is?

Want to know more about canoeing?
Visit American Canoe Association at www.americancanoe.org

Cycling

Olympic cycling is a highly diverse sport made up of 22 events in five disciplines — road, track, mountain, BMX freestyle and BMX racing. While each discipline is different and requires a unique set of skills, many cyclists compete across multiple disciplines.

How the Sport Began

The first, two-wheeled bike had no pedals and had to be pushed by foot. It is thought to have originated in central Germany in the early 19th century; pedals were added in 1861. Early designs had a large front wheel with small rear wheels and were dangerous. In 1885, an English company invented the safety bike — its wheels were the same size and had a chain connecting the pedals to the wheels. Cycling was included in the first Olympic Games in 1896.

CYCLING BROADCAST SCHEDULE

BMX		Mountain		Road		
7/30	8/1	7/26	7/27	7/24	7/25	7/28

Track						
8/2	8/3	8/4	8/5	8/6	8/7	8/8

Watch all of the action on the networks of NBCUniversal including

CNBC

Understanding the Sport

Mountain biking, the road race, and BMX racing all have the goal to be the first to the finish line. While the starting formats, course designs, and equipment vary, each rider competes against other riders directly.

BMX freestyle is similar to freestyle skiing, snowboarding, or skateboarding. Each athlete is awarded points based on the difficulty of their 'tricks' and the athlete with the highest point total is the winner.

Track cycling events take place in a velodrome — an indoor, oval track with steeply banked turns. Events include the keirin (riders follow a pacer at 30-50 kph) and the omnium (combination of 4 races).

Scan me for more!

Track the Medals

Tokyo Olympic Qualifier

Roberts was the first American to qualify in BMX freestyle for the US. She began riding at 9 following in the footsteps of her cousin, top BMX cyclist Brett Banasiewicz.

Who's Competing?

Follow your favorite athletes.

NAME	SCORE/TIME

Did You Know?

The first bike race took place in 1868 — only seven years after pedals were invented!

Fun Facts

The first Tour de France took place in 1903 and covered 1,450 miles!

Wilbur and Orville Wright (The Wright Brothers) originally owned a bike repair shop.

Many of Henry Ford's production methods for the first cars were inspired by early bicycle manufacturing.

Cycling

Word Scramble

MERB ______________________

GDBIRE ______________________

RDYNE ______________________

GFRIATND ______________________

EFLYR ______________________

HETHOSLO ______________________

TPNEOLO ______________________

GTELKNACRIS ______________________

RTSNAKATDC ______________________

VMREDOLOE ______________________

Name that Pictogram

The sport of cycling is made up of five distinct disciplines: BMX Freestyle, BMX Racing, Mountain Biking, Road Biking, and Track Racing. Fill in the correct discipline next to each pictogram.

 ______________________

 ______________________

 ______________________

 ______________________

 ______________________

Compare & Contrast

Compare and contrast the differences between each of the cycling events.

____

____

____

____

____

____

____

____

Discussion Questions

1. BMX freestyle is a new event this year. What tricks are you excited to see performed?
2. Each discipline has a unique bicycle style. Can you describe the differences in each bicycle?
3. European cyclists have been strong contenders in traditional events, while non-European countries fare better in BMX. Why do you think that is?

Diving

Diving is the sport of jumping or falling into water from a platform or springboard, usually while performing acrobatics. Diving is an internationally recognized sport that's also part of the Olympic Games.

How the Sport Began

Diving has been practiced for thousands of years. The first historical record — dating back to 480 BCE — is a painting of a male diver found in a burial chamber south of Naples, Italy. Competitive diving began in Great Britain in 1883 with the first "plunging" competition. The goal of plunging was to travel as far up the pool as possible while remaining motionless and face down. The first modern-era diving competition was held in Scotland in 1889.

Track the Medals

Tokyo Olympic Hopeful

Four time Olympic medalist, Boudia has been part of the US National Diving team since age 16. At the London Games, he defeated hometown favorite Tom Daley to take the gold.

DIVING BROADCAST SCHEDULE

3M Springboard

7/25 7/28 8/1 8/3

10M Platform

7/26 7/27 8/5 8/7

Watch all of the action on the networks of NBCUniversal including

Understanding the Sport

Most diving competitions consist of three disciplines: 1-meter springboard, 3-meter springboard, and the platform.

In platform events, competitors perform their dives on either the 5, 7 ½, 9, or 10-meter towers. In major diving meets, including the Olympic Games and the World Championships, platform diving is from the 10-meter height.

All men's events have 6 dives per competition phase and all women's events have 5.

Who's Competing?

Follow your favorite athletes.

NAME	SCORE

Scan me for more details about Diving!

Fun Facts

Nearly two decades after his 1984 and 1988 gold medal performances, Greg Louganis was featured on the iconic Wheaties box.

Diving first appeared at the Olympics at the 1904 Games in St. Louis.

Diving was known as "fancy diving" for the acrobatic stunts performed by divers (including somersaults and twists).

Did You Know?

Judges score dives without consulting each other or watching video replays.

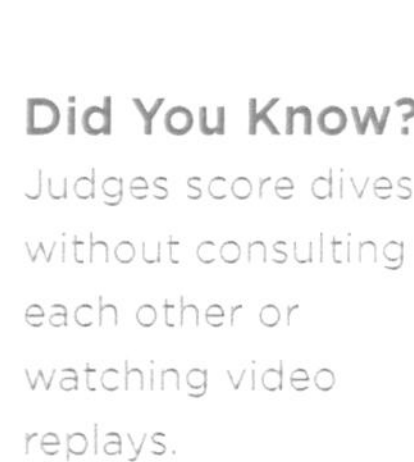

Word Search

W A B T A K B U I C P Y A C P
B C R A E P F P I K E L A L Z
Y S E M C X P Y C V Z J N T A
X H I C S K E R J L V Y Y J O
N A I Q H T W C O H H Q S Q C
P C H B I K A A U A R U X V T
K D R D U M P N R T C N I C U
I R J I A E B A D D I H E C C
J P L A T F O R M D D O U B K
S E M C J U I J R K I I N U Y
C W H W F Y U S V R R V V E C
W A V H X F Q R S Q C Y E E C
S P R I N G B O A R D G D J H
Z E M G U D H M B G I M Y C M
F X S C S O M E R S A U L T B

APPROACH	EXECUTION	SOMERSAULT
ARMSTAND DIVE	PIKE	SPRINGBOARD
BACKWARD DIVE	PLATFORM	TUCK

Discussion Questions

1. Often divers are accomplished gymnasts or dancers. Why do you think that is?
2. When doing a summersault in a tuck position, divers hold tightly to their legs. What advantage do you think that gives them?

Compare & Contrast

Olympic diving is done from either a platform or a springboard. Describe some of the differences you see between the two types of diving.

Diving

Name the Position

All dives are based on four distinct body positions. Can you name them all below?

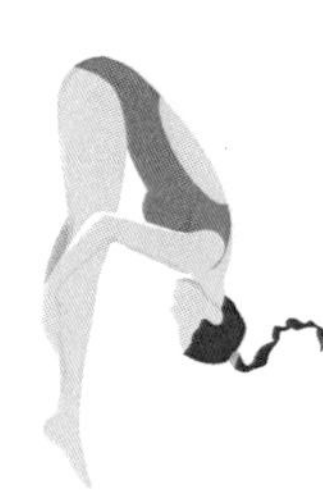

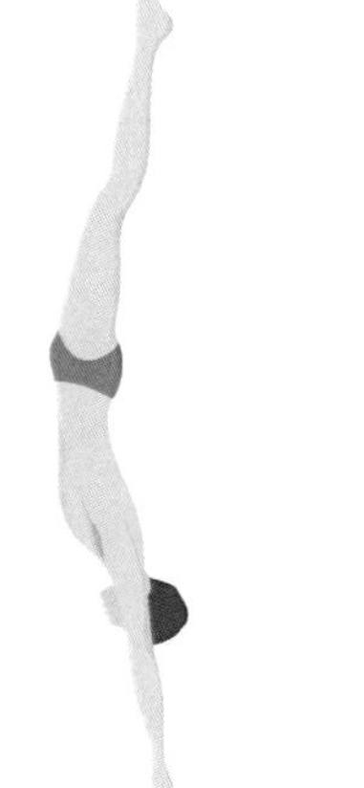

Want to know more about Diving?
Visit USA Diving at www.teamusa.org/usa-diving

Equestrian

Equestrian, or horseback riding, is referred to the skill of riding with horses. Equestrian activities can be both recreational and competitive.

How the Sport Began

Equestrian sports developed in the second half of the 19th century. On April 15, 1868, the Royal Dublin Society included two jumping events — the "high leap" and the "wide leap" — on the program of its annual horse show.

Equestrian was first included in the Olympics at the 1900 Games in Paris with three equestrian events: show jumping, the high jump, and the long jump.

Understanding the Sport

Equestrian is the only Olympic sport with no gender distinction in any event. Men and women compete together in all 6 events.

The following are part of the equestrian events at the Olympics.

Dressage: horses perform a series of pre-arranged movements to show responsiveness to the rider's commands.

Eventing: a test of total horsemanship. This discipline is broken up into 3 parts: dressage, a cross-country course with obstacles, and jumping.

Jumping: involves clearing obstacles in a specified time without any faults.

Scan me for more!

Track the Medals

Beijing Olympic Medalist

Equestrian athlete, Canadian Ian Miller, competed in 10 Olympics--the record for most Olympic appearances!

Who's Competing?

Follow your favorite athletes.

NAME	SCORE

EQUESTRIAN BROADCAST SCHEDULE

Dressage		Eventing	Jumping	
7/27	7/28	8/2	8/4	8/7

Watch all of the action on the networks of NBCUniversal including

Did You Know?

Because it involves dressage, a cross-country race and jumping, eventing is considered the most physically demanding Olympic equestrian discipline.

Fun Facts

The horses of the medal-winning athletes receive ribbons as a prize.

Art from around the world shows humans have ridden horseback since pre-historic times.

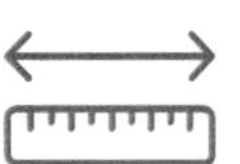

The 1900 Summer Olympics was the only Games to date to feature an equestrian long jump competition.

Crossword

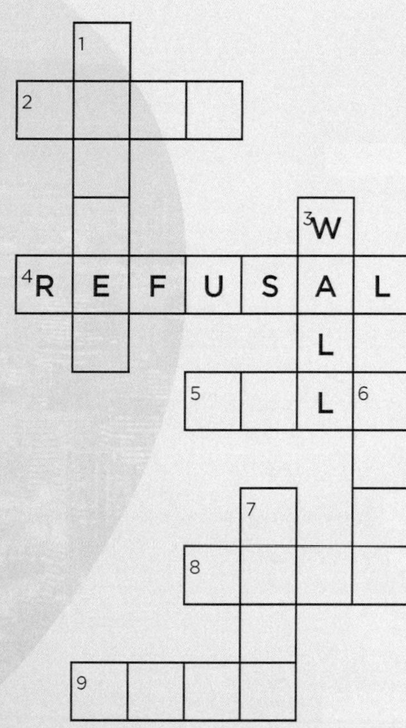

DOWN

1 A gait, which resembles but is slower than a full gallop, when three legs are simultaneously off the ground

3 A type of jump constructed of wooden blocks, which are traditionally painted to resemble stone

6 A gait in which the horse moves its diagonal legs at the same pace

7 A marching pace in which the footfalls of the horse's feet follow one another in "four time."

ACROSS

2 A white strip on the edge of the water jump

4 When a horse stops at a jump, incurring faults

5 When the horse stands attentive and motionless, with all four legs straight and even to each other.

8 The four movements used by a horse: walk, trot, canter and gallop

9 To stop short of an obstacle

Equestrian

Compare & Contrast

Compare and contrast the differences between each of the events.

Discussion Questions

1. Eventing is considered the most demanding Olympic discipline. Which part do you think is the most challenging?

2. Horse breeds come in all shapes and sizes. Which breeds do you think fare the best in equestrian events?

Name that Pictogram

There are three disciplines in Equestrian - Dressage, Eventing, and Jumping. Can you match them to the correct pictogram?

Fencing

Fencing is the organized sport involving the use of a sword for attack and defense, according to set movements and rules. Although the use of swords dates to prehistoric times and swordplay to ancient civilizations, modern fencing began in the 19th century and it has become a lifelong sport for people of all ages & backgrounds.

How the Sport Began

The history of fencing goes back at least three millennia; its earliest documented depiction is on an Egyptian temple that dates to about 1190 BCE.
Although fencing was practiced in Colonial America, modern fencing came to the U.S. in the 1840s. The world's first national governing body for fencing was the Fencers League of America (now the USA Fencing). The first national championships were held in 1888.

Track the Medals

TOKYO 2020

FENCING BROADCAST SCHEDULE

Foil		Epée		Sabre	
7/25	7/26	7/24	7/25	7/24	7/26
7/29	8/1	7/27	7/30	7/28	7/31

Watch all of the action on the networks of NBCUniversal including

Understanding the Sport

Fencing events take place between two competitors, and are primarily based on striking your opponent with a blunt weapon while avoiding attacks. A significant breadth of rules govern when and how hitting an opponent scores a point and varies between the 3 weapons: foil, sabre, and épée. Each sword has unique strategies with little crossover of style between disciplines. There are both individual and team events in fencing. Individually, the winner is the first to 15 points, or the fencer with the most points when time expires. In the team event, the goal is to reach 45 points as a team before your opponent.

Tokyo Olympic Qualifier

Three time Olympic medalist, also was the Parade of Nations flag bearer for the 2012 London Olympic Games.

Fun Facts

Fencing suits are white because touching was originally recorded with a piece of cotton at the sword's tip and dripped in ink.

Fencing is the only Olympic combat sport with no weight classes.

Fencing is one of five sports to be included in every Olympic program since 1896, along with cycling, swimming, gymnastics, and track and field.

Who's Competing?

Follow your favorite athletes.

NAME	SCORE

Scan me for more details about Fencing!

Did You Know?

President Theodore Roosevelt and Winston Churchill were former fencers.

Word Scramble

EADNAVC ______________________

EZLAL ______________________

BTOU ______________________

EN ERDAG ______________________

ETIFN ______________________

GLUNE ______________________

YRPAR ______________________

EIPST ______________________

RPSEIOT ______________________

TSHUTR ______________________

Discussion Questions

1. Each sword has a unique shape. Which one do you think is more challenging to master?
2. Fencers commonly use either their height or their speed to win. Which do you think offers a greater advanage?
3. While foil and sabre use the rule of priority, epee does not. Why do you think that is?

Compare & Contrast

Draw a sabre, épée, and foil. What are the main differences?

DRAW SABRE HERE

____

____

____

DRAW ÉPÉÉ HERE

____

____

____

DRAW FOIL HERE

____

____

____

Want to know more about Fencing?
Visit USA Fencing at www.usafencing.org

Field Hockey

Field hockey is a sport in which two teams try to maneuver a ball into the opponent's goal using a stick. The sport is often simply referred to as hockey.

How the Sport Began

The first men's hockey club was formed around 1861. The addition of other clubs eventually led to the establishment of the Hockey Association in London in 1886. The sport gained international appeal once the Association standardized the game using rules from London's Wimbledon Hockey Club and the British army introduced the game overseas.

Understanding the Sport

Since the 1976 Montreal Olympics, all international field hockey matches have been played on synthetic turf. Players are only permitted to use the flat side of the stick to make contact with the ball.

Field hockey made its Olympic debut in 1908, and the first Olympic women's field hockey event took place in 1980.

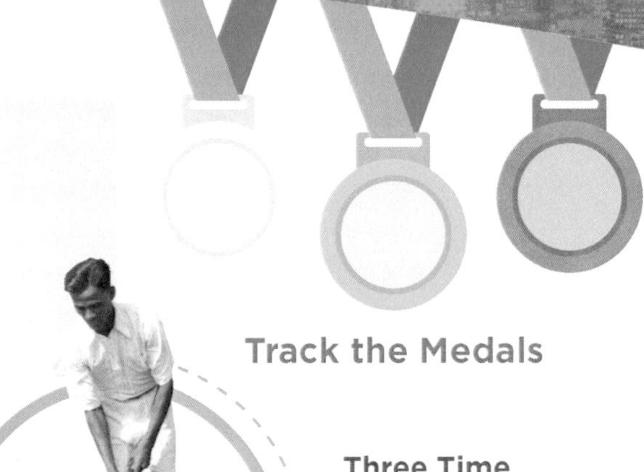

Track the Medals

Three Time Olympic Champion

Indian field hockey great, Chand won gold in 1928, 1932, and 1936. During his career he scored over 500 goals.

FIELD HOCKEY BROADCAST SCHEDULE

Men	Women
8/5	8/6

Watch all of the action on the networks of NBCUniversal including

Fun Facts

The Netherlands has been the most successful country in women's Olympic field hockey, winning a total of eight medals (three gold).

In 1908, Great Britain won four medals in the debut of Olympic men's field hockey. England (gold), Ireland (silver), Scotland and Wales (bronze) were the four semifinalists, and each of them claimed a medal for Great Britain.

India is the all-time leader with eight Olympic field hockey gold medals (all in men's field hockey).

Who's on the team?

Follow your favorite athletes.

NAME	POSITION

Scan for more about Field Hockey!

Did You Know?

Zimbabwe's only Olympic gold medal in a team sport came in women's field hockey at the 1980 Moscow Olympics.

Word Search

```
L O Q Q M T F U P G I H T Y T
L J X C B Z E N C S Z K X M A
F P N D I J Y D Z J W F J Q C
I L M A L B I E V Y D J X C K
S G I F I Y A R H Y X Q K D L
C R U C E H D C T D X T W T E
O J D C K D V U H R M Y P T B
O A R G A M A T B I A E P T U
P M Q J N Q N T S B B N B F L
S A Y G J B C I T B N Z L I L
W R F G R B I N R L H O S N Y
N K Z G J C N G I E S U K P Y
E I C X N N G G K B E C H U R
H N R K I H T C E L O T J S B
R G W H T W U X R Z C Z R H O
```

ADVANCING	MARKING	STRIKER
BULLY	PUSH	TACKLE
DRIBBLE	SCOOP	UNDERCUTTING
FLICK		

Compare & Contrast

Compare the differences between field hockey and ice hockey.

Field Hockey

Place the Players

Line up all eleven players on the pitch.

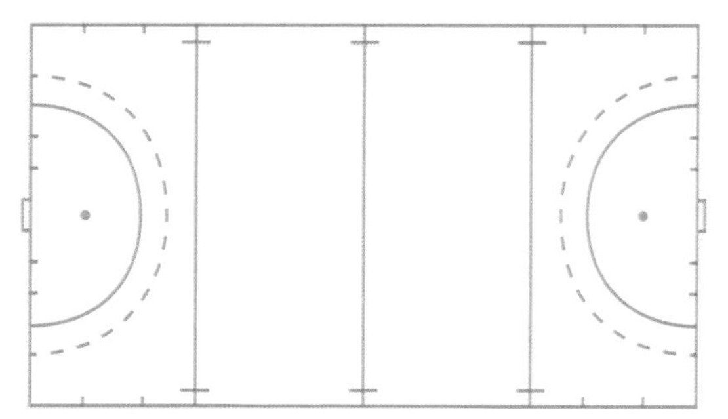

- Goalkeeper
- Defense
- Midfield
- Forward

Discussion Questions

1. Since 1976, matches have predominantly been played on artifical turf. What do you think are the advantages to turf over grass?

2. India's teams have won the most gold medals between 1908 and 1980, but not since. What factors could have allowed other countries to become more dominant?

Want to know more about Field Hockey?
Visit USA Field Hockey at www.teamusa.org/usa-field-hockey

Golf

Golf is a club-and-ball sport where players use various clubs to hit their ball into a series of holes. Each shot counts as one stroke. The goal is to get your ball into the hole in as few strokes as possible. Players encounter varied terrains with water hazards, sand traps (bunkers), and rocks. These are key challenges to the game.

How the Sport Began

Modern-day golf is considered a Scottish invention from the 15th century that gained popularity in the 19th century.

Golf made its debut at the 1900 Paris Olympic Games, held at the Compiègne Club, Paris, France. It consisted of a men's 36-hole stroke-play tournament and a women's nine-hole stroke-play tournament. After 1904, golf was removed from the Olympic program and would not return until the 2016 Rio Olympics.

Understanding the Sport

There are two individual events for golf at the Olympics — men's and women's. Each event consists of 4 rounds (72 holes) of stroke play over 4 days.

Each round is played in groups of three, who start at the first hole or the tenth hole. Scores cumulate from each round, and the player with the lowest combined score at the end wins.

The 2021 Olympics will be held at the Kasumigaseki Country Club — a private course in Kawagoe, Saitama, Japan.

The individual stroke competition for men will take place first over four days, followed by women.

Track the Medals

Danielle Kang

Tokyo Olympic Hopeful

Kang has five LGPA wins which earned her over 6 million dollars!

GOLF BROADCAST SCHEDULE

Men	Women
8/1	8/7

Watch all of the action on the networks of NBCUniversal including

Scan me for more!

Fun Facts

In 1967, Astronaut Alan Shepard, Jr. became the first person to play golf on the moon.

By winning the Olympic golf tournament, Margaret Abbott became the first female to win an Olympic event.

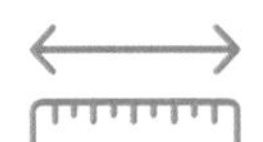

The longest drive ever recorded was 515 yards!

Did You Know?

If you walked all 18 holes on a golf course instead of riding in a cart, you would walk approximately four miles.

Name the Club

There are six different types of golf clubs, each used for different shots on the course. Can you name them?

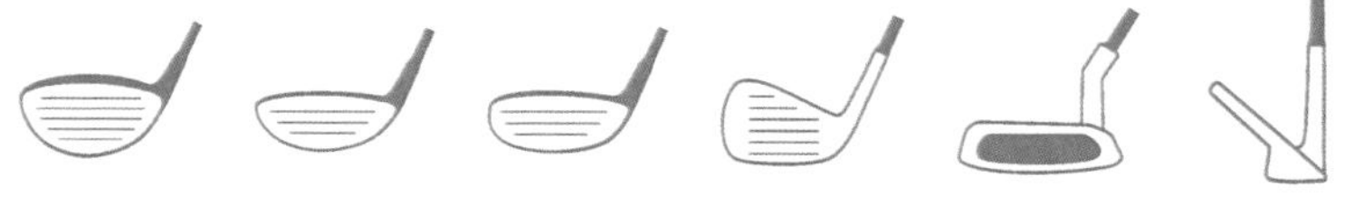

Research on Your Own

A "links" is a golf course built on land reclaimed from the ocean. St Andrews in Scotland is the oldest links in the world. What other courses around the world can be described as "links" courses?

Crossword

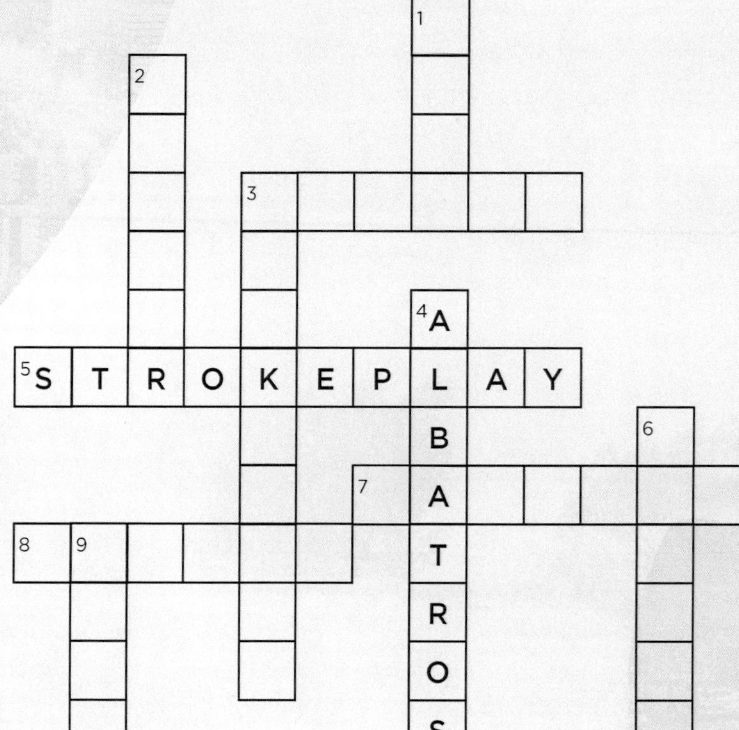

DOWN

1 A type of club that propels the ball with a lower trajectory and longer distance than an iron

2 A pit filled with sand that exists as an obstacle for the players

3 The motion where a golfer torques his/her body and club away from the ball to generate momentum to swing through the ball

4 A score of three under par on a given hole

6 An area on a course that provides a difficult obstacle, such as a water hazard or a bunker

9 A condition that causes involuntary wrist spasms when a golfer is attempting to putt

ACROSS

3 A score of one under par on a given hole

5 A form of competition based on score amassed from the number of strokes played in a given round or multiple rounds

7 This part of the course is the mowed part of any hole between the tee and the green

8 A more forgiving replacement club for long range irons, used for medium to long distance shots from the fairway

Gymnastics

Gymnastics events range from acrobatic and high-flying routines — on pommel horses, bars, and rings — to beautiful and rhythmic floor exercises. Many of the events demand a mastery of technique and a delicate grace.

How the Sport Began

Gymnastics first rose to prominence in ancient Greece as a way to prepare soldiers for battle — it kept men agile and in peak physical condition.

Educational gymnastics began in the 18th century in Germany. After designing special equipment, two physical educators created several exercises for boys, which included the parallel bars, rings, and high bars.

Track the Medals

Tokyo Olympic Hopeful

Simone Biles has 4 gymnastics moves named after her in the vault, balance beam, and 2 in floor. No other gymnast to date has done the Biles II in competition — a triple-twisting, double-tucked salto backwards.

Understanding the Sport

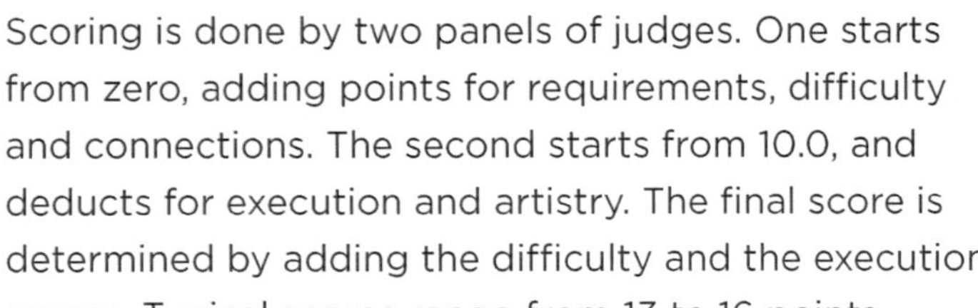

Scoring is done by two panels of judges. One starts from zero, adding points for requirements, difficulty and connections. The second starts from 10.0, and deducts for execution and artistry. The final score is determined by adding the difficulty and the execution scores. Typical scores range from 13 to 16 points.

GYMNASTICS BROADCAST SCHEDULE

Artistic

7/26 7/27 7/28 7/29 8/1 8/2 8/3

Rhythmic

8/7 8/8

Trampoline

7/30 7/31

Watch all of the action on the networks of NBCUniversal including

Fun Facts

In 1984, Mary Lou Retton was the first American woman to win an all-around gold medal.

Until the 1950s, gymnastics in the Olympics included synchronized team floor calisthenics, rope climbing, high jumping, running, and the horizontal ladder.

Many major gymnasts start their careers as early as two years old!

Who's Competing?

Follow your favorite athletes.

NAME	SCORE

Scan for more about Gymnastics!

Did You Know?

While gymnastics has been part of the Games since its inception, only men competed for the first 32 years.

Gymnastics

Word Scramble

LOFOR CSEEERIX ______

NOOZIAHTLR RBA ______

LEAAPRLL SRAB ______

GRNIS ______

LMPMEO RESHO ______

VUTNAGIL ______

ITRHHMYC VIRTESOP ______

CLANABE EMAB ______

ENNUEV SBRA ______

Name that Pictogram

There are three disciplines in the sport of gymnastics - artistic, rhythmic, and trampoline. Can you match them to the correct pictogram?

______

______

______

Athlete Bio

Who is your favorite athlete?

Describe their career & achievements.

NAME ______ AGE ______ COUNTRY ______

______

______

______

______

______

Discussion Questions

1. During the floor routines, notice how high the athletes can jump and bounce. Why do you think that is?
2. During the floor routine, listen for a bell to ring. What does that mean?
3. Notice before the pommel horse and rings and bars, the athletes put chalk on their hands. What does that help with?
4. When doing the vault, there is a line down the middle of the landing area. Why?
5. How long does each position in the rings need to be held for to be valid. What skill do the rings demonstrate?

Handball

Team handball is a game played between two teams of seven players who try to throw or hit an inflated ball into a goal at either end of a rectangular court.

How the Sport Began

Multiple reports exist regarding the founding of the modern game, it's believed that modern handball was first played near the end of the 19th century. One early game is reported to have taken place in the Danish town of Nyborg in 1897.

Understanding the Sport

Each game of handball consists of two 30-minute halves with a 15-minute halftime, and players wear no protective equipment. Each team is allowed one 60-second timeout per half. The ball is moved by passing, dribbling, or hitting it with any part of the body above the knee. In handball, only the goalkeeper may touch the ball with their feet.

The seven-man indoor game was added to the Olympic program in 1972. Women's handball became an Olympic event in 1976.

Track the Medals

Nikola Karabatić

Two Time Olympic Champion

Nicknamed the beast, Karabatić is 6'5" tall and 220 pounds. His unusual speed and agility, especially for his size, makes him one of the best handball players of all time. At 37, he is hoping to leave Tokyo with gold.

HANDBALL BROADCAST SCHEDULE

Men	Women

8/7	8/8

Watch all of the action on the networks of NBCUniversal including

Fun Facts

The size of the ball differs in men's and women's handball and is made of leather or synthetic material.

Handball combines elements of soccer, basketball, and water polo into one game.

Handball is a high scoring game; it is not uncommon to see a team score upwards of 20 times in a game.

Who's on the team?

Follow your favorite athletes.

NAME	POSITION

Scan for more about Handball!

Did You Know?

A player can't hold the ball for more than three seconds and can't move more than three steps while holding it.

Handball

Word Search

```
I G O A L T H R O W U O S G I
U C N Z A V C U I D A R A G Z
G Y L O G E O L C N E B Q J E
B K S Y U J R U A C Z T M S J
P V S V T G N G P U I H E X B
Q D T T H D E R U O C R F Y E
F I R U G R R U R W O O O B P
R V I Y M B T P W O Y W G F L
E I N Q T J H O M V Z O S P A
E N R A H Y R J R J H F S S Y
T G O N G M O C J Y J F X V M
H S E A R V W T B V Y O T K A
R H U Y E L L O W C A R D V K
O O P E N A L T Y T H R O W E
W T Z G O O A B H J A M B Q R
```

CORNER THROW	PENALTY THROW
DIVING SHOT	PLAYMAKER
FREE THROW	THROW-OFF
GOAL THROW	YELLOW CARD

Compare & Contrast

Handball is a mixture of basketball, soccer and ice hockey. Name some of the similarities to each of those sports.

____

____

____

____

____

Fact or Fiction

Circle the check mark if the statement is true, circle the 'x' if it is false.

1. In handball, it is illegal for the ball to touch a players legs.  

2. Handbll is the national sport of Wales. 

Discussion Questions

1. Handball used to be played outside on grass. What are the advantages or disadvantages of playing indoors?

2. Referees can penalize teams who play too passively. Why is that an issue for teams?

3. Players can only hold the ball for three seconds and take three steps. How far do you think you can move in three steps?

4. Shooting and scoring is similar to soccer, except you use your hands instead of feet (and a smaller goal). Which method of scoring is more challenging?

Judo

Judo was created as a physical, mental and moral exercise in Japan, in 1882, by Kanō Jigorō. It is generally categorized as a modern martial art which later evolved into a combat and Olympic sport.

How the Sport Began

Kanō Jigorō (1860–1938) collected the knowledge of the old jujitsu schools of the Japanese samurai and in 1882 founded his Kōdōkan School of judo (from the Chinese jou-tao, or roudao, meaning "gentle way").

Understanding the Sport

Judo's most prominent feature is its competitive element, where the objective is to either throw or take an opponent down to the ground, immobilize or subdue them with a pin, or force them to submit with a joint lock or a choke.

Strikes and thrusts by hands and feet as well as weapons defenses are a part of judo, but only in prearranged forms and are not allowed in competition or free practice. A judo practitioner is called a judoka.

For the Tokyo Olympics, there will be 15 events — seven weight classes for men, seven for women, and a new 'Mixed Team' event.

Scan for more details about Judo!

Track the Medals

Kayla Harrison

Two Time Olympic Champion

Harrison is also a mixed martial artist and competes in the Professional Fighters League.

Who's Competing?

Follow your favorite athletes.

NAME	SCORE

TOKYO 2020

JUDO BROADCAST SCHEDULE

Men & Women

7/24 7/25 7/26 7/27 7/28 7/29 7/30

Mixed Team

7/31

Watch all of the action on the networks of NBCUniversal including

Fun Facts

In the upcoming Tokyo Olympics, judo will be contested at the Nippon Budokan, the same venue that hosted the inaugural Olympic judo competition in 1964.

Judo was founded in 1882 by Kanō Jigorō, who trained in Jiu Jitsu.

The name Judo means the 'Gentle Way'.

Did You Know?

Japan has been the most successful nation in Olympic judo, winning 39 gold medals and 84 total medals. France is second with 14 gold and 49 total medals, while South Korea is third with 11 gold and 43 total medals.

Crossword

DOWN

1 (come to) Attention
3 Person performing a Judo technique
4 Bow
5 Bow performed from a standing posture.
7 Judo Uniform
8 Person receiving a Judo technique
9 Sitting position with legs crossed

ACROSS

2 Place or club where Judo is practiced
5 Free practice
6 Repetition practice without throwing
8 Falling practice (side, back, forward)
10 Kneeling position
11 Teacher or Instructor
12 Kneeling bow
13 Shout during execution of technique

Judo

Discussion Questions

1. Judo and wrestling are similar in that you're trying to pin your opponent into submission. Can you think of other sports that are similar?

2. Japan has traditionally dominated the sport, but France is second, before South Korea. Why do you think France does so well in competition?

Athlete Bio

Who is your favorite athlete?

Describe their career & achievements.

NAME ______

AGE ______ COUNTRY ______

______

______

______

______

______

Karate

Karate is both a martial art and a sport. Kumite, the fighting discipline, involves kicking and punching techniques performed on permitted parts of the body against an opponent, while kata, the demonstration discipline, emphasizes strength, grace and speed.

How the Sport Began

Karate evolved in East Asia over a period of centuries, becoming systematized in Okinawa in the 17th century. It was brought to Japan in the 1920s. Several schools and systems have developed, each favoring different techniques and training methods.

Karate, like other Asian martial arts disciplines, stresses mental attitude, rituals of courtesy, costumes, and a complex ranking system (by belt color).

Understanding the Sport

Karate will make its debut at the Tokyo Olympics in 2021 and will feature two types of events: Kumite and Kata. Kumite, the fighting discipline, is predominantly a striking art through punching and kicking techniques. Athletes aim to score higher than their opponents during kumite matches. Kata, the demonstration discipline, is a performance of pre-defined movements in front of judges.

Kumite will feature 60 competitors from around the world across 6 events (3 for men, 3 for women), and 20 will compete in Kata (2 events, 1 for each gender).

Track the Medals

Tokyo Olympic Qualifier

Advice to younger athletes: There will be times where you just want to give up, but hard work pays off. Stay focused, surround yourself with good people and the results will come naturally.

KARATE BROADCAST SCHEDULE

Men & Women

8/5 8/6 8/7

Watch all of the action on the networks of NBCUniversal including

Scan for more details about Karate!

Did You Know?

Okinawa, Japan, is known as the home and birthplace of karate, though it was influenced by Chinese martial arts.

Fun Facts

In addition to becoming stronger, karate helps you to work on your focus, discipline, agility, and flexibility.

The place or hall where karate is practiced is known as a "dojo." Teachers are called "sensei."

In kumite, competitors earn the most points for "Ippon," either kicking the face, head or neck of their opponent or sending their opponent off their feet.

Karate

Word Search

L F O W E X F Z P L Q S W B I
V F I P F V T F T E Q I U N D
K A J V D H U X F A T O C B O
A R J V O S A I G P T X H Q M
K I K I Z A U J E W W A I W O
A F J I O D S V I E D J M O A
T Z F Y O Z E A D M W F Q I R
O X H U X T E B Y L E R K F I
W N R N A E S P O O T E J W G
G E P U W M Q U I O N S Z D A
M W F R A Y K F K M G A U S T
O M H R C B O I A E I M R K O
J P T W E F P D M S E M P A I
T A E B D V X S B E X T V O J
J X Z Z Y E E E K E F I P M M

KIOTSUKE
HAJIME
KIME
SAYONARA
KAKATO
TATAMI
DOZO
TSUKI
SEMPAI
UCHI
DOMO ARIGATO

Compare & Contrast

Can you explain the main difference between karate and taekwondo?

____

____

____

Athlete Bio

Who is your favorite athlete?

Describe their career & achievements.

NAME ______________ AGE ____ COUNTRY ________

____

____

____

____

____

____

____

Discussion Questions

1. Karate is entering the Olympics for the first time! Which discipline are you more excited to watch? Why?
2. Kumite competitions are scored similar to fencing and boxing. Of these disciplines, which do you think has a more challenging point system?

Modern Pentathlon

A pentathlon is a collection of five sports rolled into a single competition. The five events in the modern pentathlon — fencing, swimming, horse riding, pistol shooting, and running — were chosen to reflect skills that cavalry soldiers of the 19th-century should possess and refine.

How the Sport Began

The events included in modern pentathlon were chosen by this logic: a soldier is ordered to deliver a message before battle. The soldier mounts the horse and gallops off, clearing any obstacles in the way. The soldier then dismounts and fights through enemy patrols with a sword and pistol, then swims across a river and runs through the woods to accomplish the mission.

Track the Medals

Tokyo Olympic Qualifier

Elgeziry comes from a family of Olympians. His wife & brother Omar are active Olympians and his brother Emad is an Olympic legend.

Understanding the Sport

The modern pentathlon event includes combat sports (fencing), aquatic sports (swimming), equestrian sports (show jumping), athletic sports (cross-country running), and target sports (shooting).

Athletes gain points for their performance in each event. These scores are combined to give the overall total. In the modern pentathlon, starting times for the last event are staggered. Before the last event, competitors are ranked according to their score from the other disciplines and given start times accordingly, with the leader going first. The first person to cross the finish line is the overall points leader and wins the pentathlon.

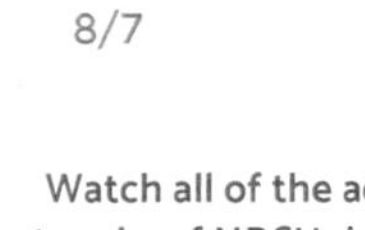

MODERN PENTATHLON
BROADCAST SCHEDULE

Men	Women
8/7	8/6

Watch all of the action on the networks of NBCUniversal including

Who's Competing?

Follow your favorite athletes.

NAME	SCORE/TIME

Scan for more details about Modern Pentathlon!

Did You Know?

In modern pentathlons, successful athletes are required to have a wide variety of skills across vastly different sports as opposed to the decathlon which utilizes the same few skills (speed, strength, and endurance).

Fun Facts

The youngest gold medalist was Anatoly Starostin from the USSR. At 20, he won gold at the 1980 Moscow Olympics.

The event was designed to showcase the skills needed by cavalry behind enemy lines.

Until 1952, only military officers could compete in the pentathlon. Sweden's Lars Hall was the first civillian gold medalist.

Modern Pentathlon

Word Search

K A U Z Q J V N I S R M V D B
C X W C A I X L N X T J E X P
G E E S H S S U A W F R I K R
Y C Q D V H I C M N X E K J Q
T A O T F G F G K N A M L C I
W L B M R Q B T H E N I H U U
C L X H P N Q O E T Y S U W S
Y A B L S O R Y R D E E M F X
A G N I I O U I S E T R T P Y
Z T D T J L W N W W O H S I H
H L X C E V K Z D I U M X S F
W A N B S R K F L E C H E T A
H T P I H H P L F G H O N E U
Z H K M W X Z J G M I D D S L
E P O Y D D H U Q X X F H S T

BORE	FLECHE	REMISE
CANTER	LATH	SIGHTERS
COMPOUND	PISTE	TOUCH
FAULT		

Modern Pentathlon Maze

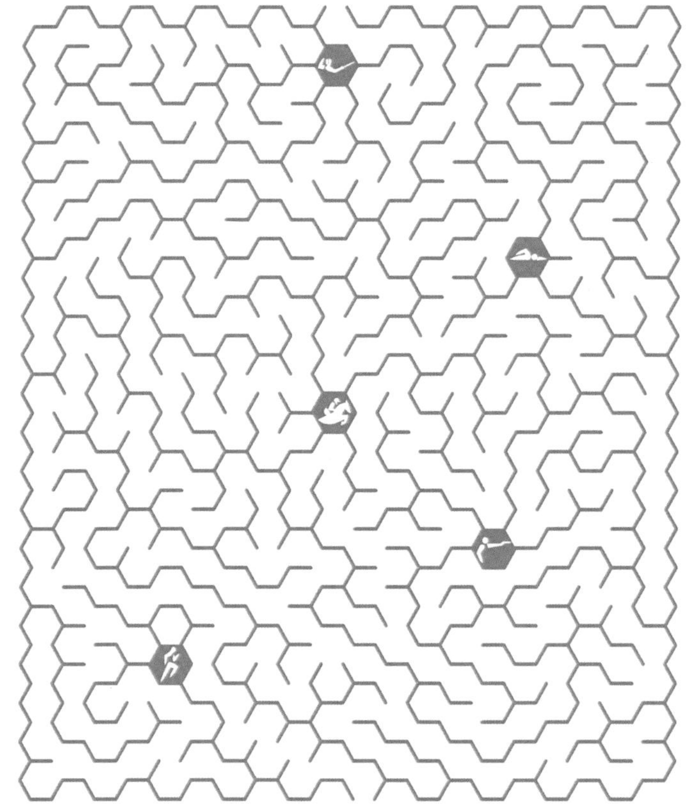

Discussion Questions

1. Modern Pentathlon was originally limited to military officers. Why do you think that was?
2. Think about each of the five events. Which one do you think is the most challenging? Which one do you think is the easiest? Why?

Rowing

Rowing is the sport of moving a boat as fast as possible on top of the water. Athletes move the boat forward by using two oars (in sculling events) or one oar (in sweep events).

How the Sport Began

Rowing has a long history due to its utility in both warfare and transportation. Rowing events were supposed to be held at the 1896 Olympics in Athens, but bad weather forced a cancellation. Men's rowing made its Olympic debut on the Seine River at the 1900 Paris Games and has been part of the Olympics ever since. Women's rowing was added in 1976.

ROWING BROADCAST SCHEDULE

Men	Women
8/7	8/8

Watch all of the action on the networks of NBCUniversal including

Understanding the Sport

The different types of rowing depend on how many people are in the boat and how many oars each rower has. There are two styles of rowing: sweep, where competitors each use a single oar, and sculling, where they use two oars placed on each side of the boat. A rowing competition is called a regatta.

Rowing features a total of 14 events (7 each for both men and women). Events include categories for open weight and restricted weight (lightweight) athletes, and there are events for single rowers, pairs, groups of four, and groups of eight. All Olympic races take place on a 2000-meter course.

Track the Medals

Kara Kohler

Tokyo Olympic Qualifier

Bronze medalist Kohler started her sports career as a swimmer. She didn't start rowing until she started college at UC-Berkley.

Fun Facts

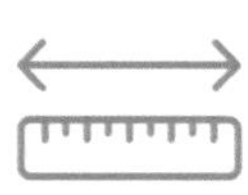

Eight-oared shells are about 62 feet long — that's more than 20 yards on a football field!

From 2006 to 2016, the U.S. won eight consecutive world titles and three consecutive Olympic gold medals in the women's eights event.

Rowing is the oldest intercollegiate sport in the United States - it was contested for the first time between Harvard and Yale in 1852.

Who's on the team?

Follow your favorite athletes.

NAME	POSITION

Scan for more about Rowing!

Did You Know?

The eight-person events are the only ones that include a coxswain, who is responsible for steering the boat from the stern (back).

Travel by Math

Find the fastest way to row from Greece to Japan. Move from square to square horizontally or vertically, but not diagonally.

Greece	7	6	1
6	9	3	7
8	5	4	Japan

Compare & Contrast

What are the advantages and disadvantages to each event?

Rowing

Crossword

4 FEATHERING

5 HATCHET

DOWN

1 A wide collar on the oar that keeps it from slipping through the oarlock

3 The flat end of the oar that is in the water during the drive

5 An innovation in the shape of the oar blade that entered the sport in 1991

6 Not a paddle. Used to drive the boat forward

8 The part of the shell at the bow and stern that is covered with fiberglass cloth or a thin plastic

ACROSS

2 The water swirls left by oars in stroke

4 Holding the blades in a flat position between strokes to reduce wind resistance during recovery

7 Not an oar. Describes rowing with very little power on the oar

9 Person who steers the shell and directs the race plan, acting as the eyes of the crew

10 The boat

Rugby

Rugby Is a contact sport developed in the early 19th century. Players carry the ball from one end of the field to the other while laterally passing between teammates. While it's similar to modern American football, rugby players don't wear protective padding and play is more continuous and closer to modern soccer.

How the Sport Began

Rugby was developed and named after the Rugby School in England. Legend has it that a student named William Webb Ellis elected to run with the ball rather than kicking it, paving the way for a new sport to emerge. Rugby sevens, the variant of the sport now used in Olympic competition, was invented in 1883 in Scotland when a local town could not afford its 15-a-side team and instead created a new competition with seven players on the field for each team.

Understanding the Sport

Rugby sevens is played on a field by 2 teams of 7 players. The objective is to obtain more points than the opposing team within 14 minutes of playing time (20 for games in which medals are awarded). Points are gained through scoring tries (rugby's equivalent to touchdowns) or kicking drop goals and penalties (similar to field goals).

Each end of the playing field has a field goal made of poles shaped like the letter "H." Around the field goal is an area called the in-goal. If a player touches the ball in the in-goal, they score a try. A drop goal or penalty is scored when a player kicks the ball through the top of the field goal.

Track the Medals

Martin Iosefo

Tokyo Olympic Hopeful

At the 2016 London Sevens, Iosefo scored a try 11 seconds into the match, one of the fastest tries in the World Series.

Scan me for more details about Rugby!

TOKYO 2020

RUGBY BROADCAST SCHEDULE

Men	Women
7/28	7/31

Watch all of the action on the networks of NBCUniversal including

Did You Know?

Since 1905, the same whistle has been used to start the game at every Rugby World Cup. It is called the Gil Evans Whistle, and it was also used at the 1924 Paris Olympics.

Fun Facts

Fiji won the 2016 Olympic gold medal in men's rugby, the first Olympic medal of any color for the small island nation.

The World Rugby Sevens Series serves as the annual global circuit for the best rugby sevens players. The men's series was founded in 1999 and women's in 2012.

Rugby has only been played as an Olympic sport five times: 1900, 1908, 1920, 1924, and 2016. The most recent is the only rugby sevens style (7-a-side).

Rugby

Word Scramble

ETENRC ______

INSOCROEVN ______

ROPD IKCK ______

LAEEGS ______

EKOHRO ______

LUMA ______

UKCR ______

RMUCS ______

TRY ______

WNIG ______

Compare & Contrast

Can you spot the rugby influences in American football?

______

______

______

Fact or Fiction

Circle the check mark if the statement is true, circle the 'x' if it is false.

1. Halftime is only two minutes long in rugby sevens. ✓ ✗
2. Canadian footbll and rugby sevens are really the same game ✓ ✗

Discussion Questions

1. Rugby is sort of a combination of soccer and American football. Can you describe which parts of these sports appear in rugby?
2. Even though rugby players don't wear much padding, they also don't suffer many injuries. Why do you think that is?
3. Before its recent debut in 2016, rugby hadn't been played in the Olympics since 1924. Why do you think it was left out for so long?

Sailing

Sailing has a long history in the Olympic Games. The sport made its debut in 1900 and, with the exception of 1904, it has appeared at every Olympic Games since then. The sport's name was changed from 'yachting' to 'sailing' at the 2000 Sydney Games.

How the Sport Began

Sailing competitions have been held since the 19th century, although these events initially didn't have any uniform set of rules. After the Netherlands popularized the sport, they gave a yacht as a gift to Charles II in England in 1660. This helped popularize sailing in England, and after sailing expanded to the American colonies, world competitions began.

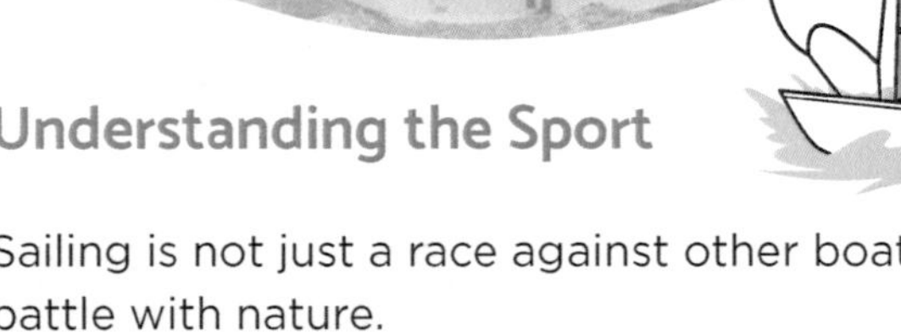

Track the Medals

Understanding the Sport

Sailing is not just a race against other boats—it's a battle with nature.

Boats cannot sail in a straight line along each leg of the course. When sailing upwind, boats must catch the wind by moving in a zig-zag pattern. Navigating the course requires changes in direction and tight turns, with crews controlling their vessels by changing the position and orientation of their bodies.

The 2021 Tokyo sailing competition will have six classes—four of them (Laser, Windsurfer, 470, and 49er) have both men's and women's competitions. The Nacra 17 has evolved to become a fully foiling boat, which means it literally flies above the water.

Scan me for more!

Tokyo Olympic Qualifier

Paige was inspired and encouraged by her older brother Zach, a 2008 Olympic silver medalist in the Finn class.

SAILING BROADCAST SCHEDULE

Men & Women

7/31 8/1 8/2 8/4

Mixed Team

8/3

Watch all of the action on the networks of NBCUniversal including

Who's Competing?

Follow your favorite athletes.

NAME	TIME

Fun Facts

The world-record sailing speed is 65.45 knots (75 mph).

The ideal wind speed for safe, comfortable sailing is generally between five and 12 knots.

Sailing has been a part of every Olympics since 1908.

Did You Know?

Sailing westward around the world is more difficult than eastward.

Sailing

Word Search

```
S X T Y I H U G P Q F A J N M
D L J L C Z E M Q C K W C O H
R L W Z Q E P L A I Z A A E S
D S E G B Z B D M S G R Q Z A
B X R I F X M I I S T W E Q Z
O P K A G T X K L N M T Z T Y
O J K E T W F O T G G A H X E
M K B F E X J I B I E H N E B
C K C C B L V K C Y T O Y D K
N O P O R L Y G M M X C G U W
W A B D O S T X Y U Q C C J M
U Y V D W F F B A C K S T A Y
Q H D D P B V B E A M Y G T N
P K C R I G G I N G O T R D Z
W L H N S P E R W N P W S R N
```

BACKSTAY
BEAM
BILGE
BOOM
DINGHY
HELMSMAN
JIB
KEEL
MAST
RIGGING

Discussion Questions

1. Sailing has six events, with both individual and team events. Can you think of advantages for individuals over teams, or vice versa?

2. Unlike other racing competitions, sailing courses are triangular. Why do you think that is?

Compare & Contrast

Compare and contrast the differences between each of the events.

____

____

____

Name the Elements

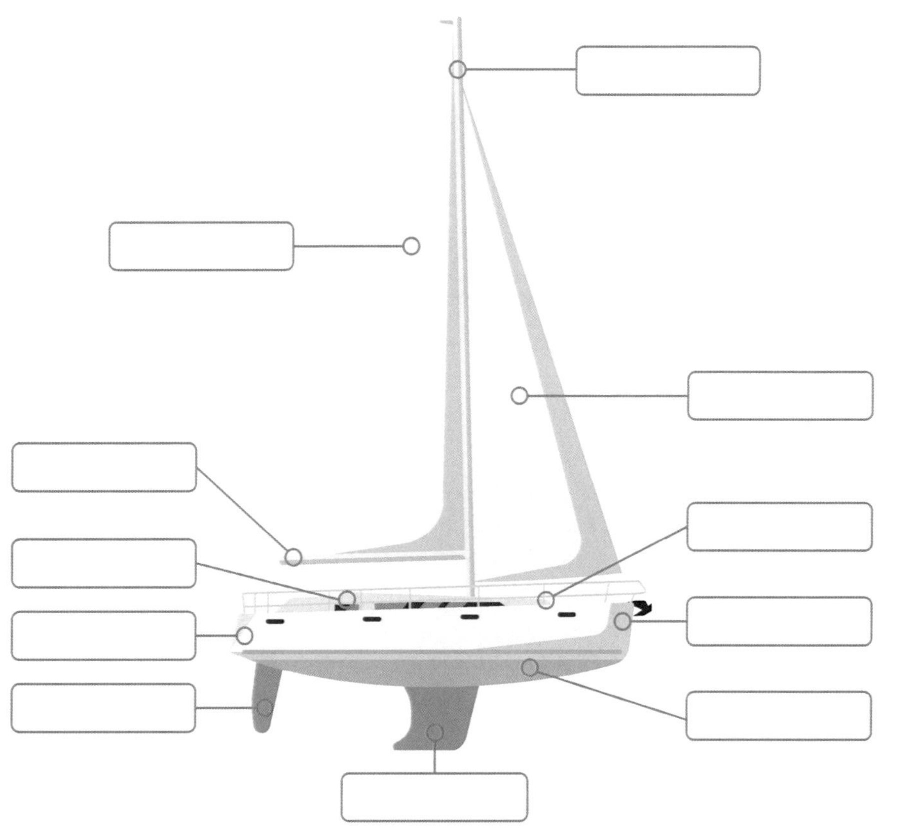

Shooting

Shooting is the sport of firing at targets with rifles, pistols, and shotguns as an exercise in marksmanship.

How the Sport Began

In the 1790s, Americans developed match rifles with long barrels and double-set trigger mechanisms. Formal match shooting emerged in 1825, and trapshooting contests followed five years later. Around the same time, competitors began to organize national federations. The first major international shooting competition was the 1896 Athens Games. The first world championships were held in France one year later.

Track the Medals

Understanding the Sport

Shooting has three main disciplines divided by gun type — rifle and pistol, where athletes shoot at stationary targets in a range, and shotgun, where athletes shoot at moving clay targets on an outdoor range.

In Tokyo, there will be four individual medal events competed for each type of gun, plus a newly-added mixed team event for all three gun types (totaling 5 events per gun, 15 events total). Each shooting event consists of a qualification round and a progressive elimination-style final round.

Tokyo Olympic Qualifier

Mary started her shooting career by watching vidoes on YouTube and using other online resources.

SHOOTING BROADCAST SCHEDULE

Men		Women		Mixed Team	
7/24	7/25	7/24	7/25	7/27	7/31
7/26	7/29	7/26	7/29		
8/2		7/30	7/31		

Watch all of the action on the networks of NBCUniversal including

Who's Competing?

Follow your favorite athletes.

NAME	SCORE

Scan for more information about Shooting!

Did You Know?

Aside from shotguns, most sport guns don't look like others you might see privately owned or depicted in pop culture.

Fun Facts

The oldest-ever Olympic medalist was a shooter - Sweden's Oscar Swahn, who won a silver medal in 1920 at age 72.

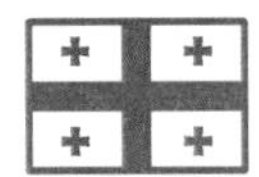

In Tokyo, three-time Olympic pistol medalist Nino Salukvadze will become the first woman in any sport to compete at 9 Olympics.

Pigeons were targets in the 1900 Games–the only time animals were ever used this way.

Name the Gun

There are six guns used in the Olympic shooting events. Can you name them all?

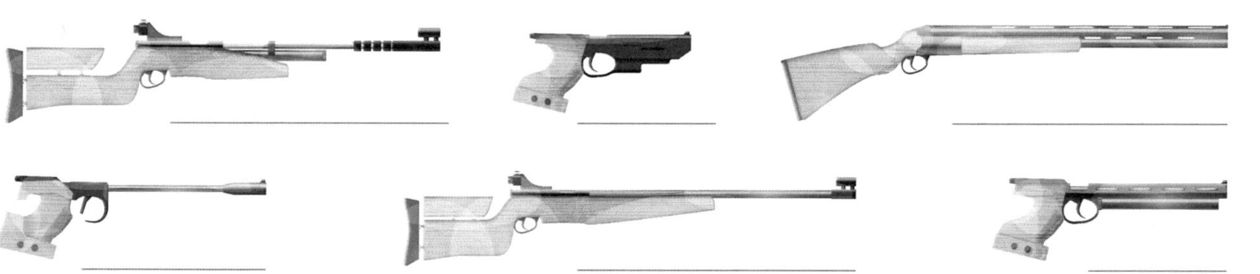

Crossword

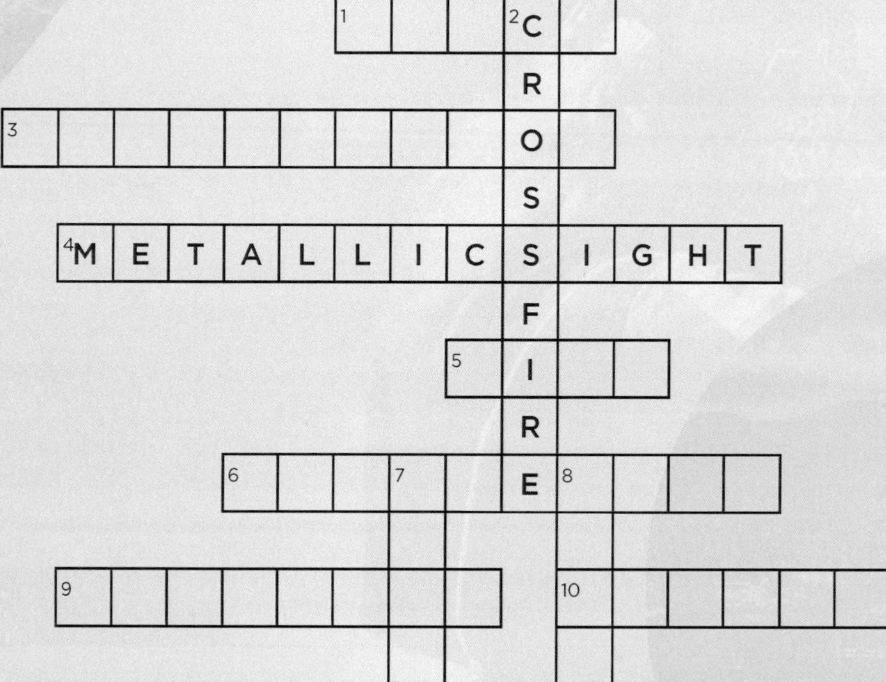

DOWN

2 A shot accidentally fired on a target assigned to another competitor
7 The interior diameter of a gun barrel
8 The device used for launching clay targets into the air

ACROSS

1 The wooden, metal, plastic or fiberglass portion of a rifle or shotgun to which the barrel, action, trigger action, etc., are attached
3 A gun or ammunition's failure to perform; not firing when the trigger is released
4 Non-magnifying devices on the front and rear ends of a firearm used to assist aim
5 In .22-caliber shooting, the area downrange where targets are placed for use
6 Competition in which two clay targets are launched simultaneously in front of the shooter
9 Practice shots fired at the beginning of a match to check sight adjustments
10 A rifle or pistol that uses compressed air or carbon dioxide to discharge metallic pellets

Want to know more about Shooting?
Visit USA Shooting at www.usashooting.org

Skateboarding

A skateboard is a short, narrow board with two small wheels attached to the bottom of either end. Skateboarders ride them and perform tricks including jumps (ollies), flips, and mid-air spins. The sport of skateboarding will make its Olympic debut at the Tokyo Olympics.

How the Sport Began

It wasn't until the 1950s when the modern skateboard–a wooden board with metal wheels–came into existence. In 1959, the first commercial skateboard appeared. It was initially marketed as 'sidewalk surfing.' It wasn't until 1973 when polyurethane wheels were introduced that the sport really took off. These wheels gripped the pavement allowing for complicated tricks. It was still a niche sport until it appeared on the X-Games.

SKATEBOARDING BROADCAST SCHEDULE

Street		Park	
7/25	7/26	8/4	8/5

Watch all of the action on the networks of NBCUniversal including

Understanding the Sport

There will be two disciplines on the program for skateboarding at the Tokyo Olympics: street and park. In street, competitors score points by utilizing features like jumps, rails and stairs (things one might find while skating down a street). In park, athletes skate and perform tricks in a dome-shaped bowl.

Nyjah Huston

Track the Medals

Tokyo Olympic Hopeful

Huston is the highest paid skateboarder with sponsorships from Nike, Monster Energy, Doritos, Mountain Dew, as well as several other brands.

Fun Facts

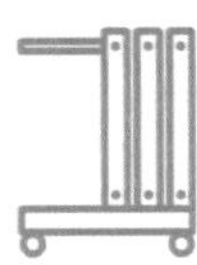

The first skateboard is said to have stemmed from a homemade wooden scooter, which became a board once the handlebars were taken off.

Skate videos helped to grow the sport once the VHS was invented in the late 1970s.

Skateboarding became more popular in the 1970s when LA residents in the middle of a drought started using drained pools to sharpen their skills.

Who's Competing?

Follow your favorite athletes.

NAME	SCORE

Scan me for more about Skateboarding!

Did You Know?

The 900 is the most demanding trick in skateboarding. It was first landed by Tony Hawk in the 1999 X-Games.

Word Scramble

AIBL ______________________

KNAB ______________________

LOBW ______________________

FAIEK ______________________

PIITLRFCK ______________________

IKCFILKP ______________________

GOYOF ______________________

LIPILSED ______________________

LILOE ______________________

LSEDI ______________________

Discussion Questions

1. Competitors receive points based on the difficulty of the tricks performed. Which tricks do think are worth the most points?
2. Park involves more aerial tricks while street traditionally has more rails. What skills would you need to practice to be proficient in both?

Compare & Contrast

Compare and contrast the main differences between street and park events.

____

____

____

____

Skateboarding

Skateboarding Maze

Soccer

The object is to kick the ball through the opponent's net. Teams move the the ball up and down the field keeping it away from the opposing team. Except during a throw-in, the other players must use their feet, knees, head and chest to control and advance the ball.

How the Sport Began

The earliest documented ancestor dates back to the 16th B.C. in China. A rock-like oval ball was used by soldiers to play the game. Other similar games existed ancient Japanese, Greek and Roman cultures, but none had the impact on modern soccer that earlier versions in the British Isles did. Little changed in the game for centuries. Then in the mid 1800s a series of innovative rules led to the meeting of the 11 London clubs and the formation of 'The Football Association.'

Understanding the Sport

The game has two 45-minute periods with a 15-minute halftime. Eleven players, ten on the field plus the goalkeeper begin the game with a kick-off by one team from the spot on the line in the midfield circle. Kick-off privileges are determined by the flip of a coin. Except for throw-ins, only the goalkeeper may play the ball with his hands or arms, and he may do so only within his own penalty area. To score, the entire ball must pass across the goal line, between the goal posts and under the crossbar.

Megan Rapinoe

Track the Medals

Tokyo Olympic Hopeful

Olympic Gold medalist, Rapinoe is known for her philanthrophy and activism. One of the first soccer players to join 'Common Goal, a campaign where athletes donate 1% of their earnings to soccer-related charities.

TOKYO 2020

SOCCER BROADCAST SCHEDULE

Men	Women
8/6	8/7

Watch all of the action on the networks of NBCUniversal including

Fun Facts

General Mills donated all proceeds from this 2019 limited edition box to two charities benefiting girls in sport.

The USWNT has dominated in women's soccer winning 4 Olympic Gold medals and 1 Silver medal.

Nigeria rallied, besting Brazil and Argentina to become the first African nation to win a soccer gold medal in 1996.

Who's on the team?

Follow your favorite athletes.

NAME	POSITION

Scan the QR code for more about Soccer!

Did You Know?

The Laws of the Game is the name of the soccer 'rule book.' It has been maintained by the International Football Association Board since 1886.

Word Search

R D R U V W Q M R M E G O N B
T E O A A Q F B A O V Y Q U Q
R W P G P A D V A N T A G E J
E J G T R C K L D K Y T Z C X
T S V R H F D D U M M Y B H Y
F L U G J R B R E A K A W A Y
H I W A L L O G U B Y F K L V
K D R N Z U L U Y H Q F O L O
C E B S J K I L G L W V V E L
T T N U T M B U S H E E B N L
C A E D A T D N Y V B T X G E
D C R R U A O C U S P A X E Y
E K V H E I X U O K C G L P O
J L A R B Y W N C Y A L Z L U
Y E J Q X O H D T H I N S V H

ADVANTAGE
BREAKAWAY
CHALLENGE
DUMMY
FIRST TOUCH
MEG
SLIDE TACKLE
THROUGH BALL
VOLLEY
WALL

Discussion Questions

1. Soccer players sometimes act injured to get a penalty call from the referees. What do you think about this behavior? Have you seen this in Tokyo?

Compare & Contrast

In soccer, a penaltiy is issued by givng a player a red card or a yellow card. Describe some of the differences between the two types of penalty cards.

Soccer

Who's on the Field?

Each soccer team has 11 players on the field at once. A typical formation usually includes four defenders, four midfielders, two forwards, and one goalkeeper. Can you identify them all?

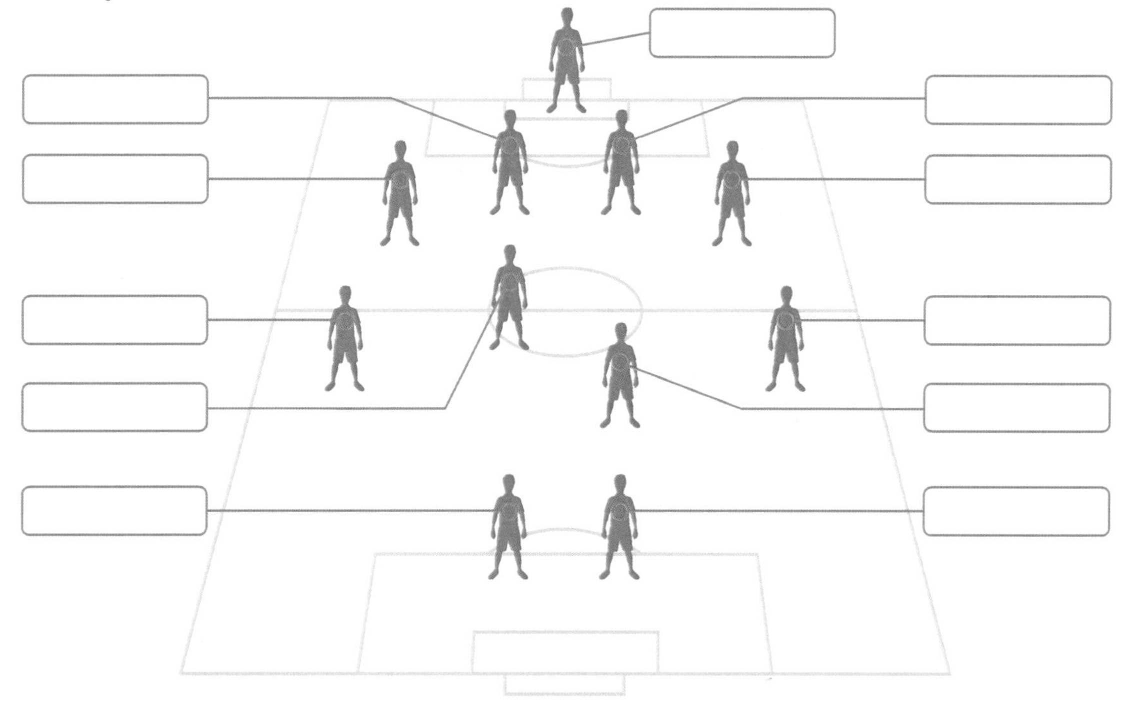

Softball

Softball is a similar game to baseball played with a larger ball (approx. 12 inch circumference) on a field with 60-foot base lengths.

How the Sport Began

Softball developed from a game called indoor baseball, first played in Chicago in 1887. It became known in the United States by various names, such as kitten ball, mush ball, diamond ball, indoor-outdoor, and playground ball. Each style had wide variances in playing rules, size, and type of playing equipment, and dimensions of the playing field.

Understanding the Sport

The fundamentals of softball are the same as baseball — batting and fielding strategies are similar, but softball is played on a much smaller field, and each game is only 7 innings long.

The ball is delivered by an underhand motion, whereas in baseball the pitch is generally overhand or sidearm.

Baseball and softball return to the Olympics for the first time since 2008, but for now, it's a one-time-only return to the program.

Track the Medals

USA 38

Cat Osterman

Tokyo Olympic Qualifer

In 2004, Cat was the youngest athlete on the Team USA softbtall team. Today, she is the oldest athlete on the team.

TOKYO 2020

SOFTBALL BROADCAST SCHEDULE

Medal Games

7/27

Watch all of the action on the networks of NBCUniversal including

Did You Know?

Organized softball sprouted after a Chicago sporting goods salesman helped convince teams to play in a 55-team single-elimination tournament in conjunction with the 1933 World's Fair in Chicago.

Scan me for more information about Softball!

Fun Facts

The U.S. has reached the gold-medal game every time softball has been contested at the Olympics, winning gold in 1996, 2000 and 2004, and silver in 2008 (losing to Japan).

Softball made its Olympic debut in 1996. Every softball game at the 1996 Atlanta Olympics was completely sold out.

There are two types of softball: slow pitch and fast pitch. Fast pitch is the type contested in the Olympics.

Softball

Word Scramble

NODARU EHT RHON ____________________

LAKB ____________________

RGEDIN ____________________

EUOBDL YPAL ____________________

LLUF CNUTO ____________________

TOH CERNRO ____________________

KLEPIC ____________________

OWREP TEIHRT ____________________

RTKESI ZONE ____________________

LKWA ____________________

Compare & Contrast

Softball and baseball are very similar sports. List 3 things that are different and 3 things that are the same.

____

____

____

Picture Math

Can you solve the equation?

bat + bat + bat = 18

catcher's mask + catcher's mask + bat = 14

ball + ball - catcher's mask = 2

catcher's mask + ball + crossed bats = ___

Discussion Questions

1. Softballs are larger and thrown underhand. What are the advantages and challenges to throwing a softball?
2. Pitchers generally favor to pitch in a windmill-style throw. Why do you think that is?
3. While the U.S. is a dominant force in softball, Japan won the most recent gold medal. With the home advantage, do you think they can repeat their victory?

Want to know more about Softball?
Visit USA Softball at www.teamusa.org/usa-softball

Sport Climbing

Sport climbing takes the challenge of scaling steep ascents to a whole new level. Using a range of hand and foot holds of different shapes and sizes, climbers put their skills and strength into practice on a vertical wall.

The wall may feature varying angles of either positive (known in climbing as a slab) or negative (steep, overhanging) sections.

How the Sport Began

Smith Rock is known as the birthplace of American sport climbing. By the early 1980s, all the big ascents had been done, and climbing pioneer Alan Watts began drilling in protection bolts to create new routes. Soon, Smith Rock turned from a local Pacific Northwest attraction into a global destination for elite climbers.

BASKETBALL BROADCAST SCHEDULE

Men	Women
8/5	8/6

Watch all of the action on the networks of NBCUniversal including

Brooke Raboutou

Track the Medals

Tokyo Olympic Qualifier

At age 9, she became the first climber to sucessfully complete a 5.13b climb–the same difficulty of The Nose of El Capitan!

Understanding the Sport

Sport climbing will make its debut at the Tokyo Games with the combined event, which features 3 disciplines: speed, bouldering, and lead. Speed climbing pits two climbers against each other, both climbing a route on a 15-meter wall in a matter of seconds. In bouldering, athletes scale a number of fixed routes on a 4-meter wall in a specified time. For Lead, athletes attempt to climb as high as possible on a wall measuring over 15 meters tall within a specified time.

The final rankings will be determined by multiplying the placement in each discipline. The athlete achieving the lowest scores wins.

Scan me for more!

Who's Competing?

Follow your favorite athletes.

NAME	TIME

Did You Know?

The first organized competition for sport climbing came in 1985, when a lead climbing event called SportRoccia was held in Bardonecchia, Italy. The following year, more than 10,000 people attended the finals.

Fun Facts

Climbing walls are now present in more than 140 countries around the world.

A study has shown that climbing is as good for cardio as running an 8-11 minute mile.

The Verdon Gorge in the French Alps is commonly referred to as the birthplace of sport climbing. The first prominent bolted route at the Verdon Gorge, Pichenibule, was completed in 1980.

Crossword

Sport Climbing

DOWN

1 A short runner used to attach a rope to a bolted anchor with carabiners.

2 A type of climbing that is usually low enough to the ground to be done without the use of ropes for safety. It can be done on the base of high climbs or on boulders.

5 A method of controlling the climbing rope that is used to prevent a climber from falling to the ground should they come off the rock.

6 A very shallow climbing hold that offers very little natural form to hold onto. The climber uses friction and tension (and sometimes sheer desperation) to make use of it.

8 When a climber uses prior knowledge and beta to ascend a route cleanly from start to finish on their first attempt, without falling.

ACROSS

3 A large handhold that is usually very secure and deep making it easy for the climber to hold onto it with confidence. A gift from the heavens!

4 A large, hollow, bolted-on bouldering hold.

7 In competition bouldering, a hold roughly half way through a boulder which counts towards scoring. Formerly known as a bonus hold.

9 When the rock is so steep that it goes beyond vertical and hangs over the ground.

10 Metal loop (usually aluminum) with a spring-loaded gate on one side used for connecting various parts of a climbing system.

Discussion Questions

1. Sport climbing is making its Olympic debut with three disciplines. Which one are you excited for? Why?

2. Speed and lead events both require athletes to use safety ropes. What are the advantages or disadvantages to having safety ropes in place?

**Want to know more about Sport Climbing?
Visit USA Climbing at www.usaclimbing.org**

Surfing

Surfing is contested in the ocean. Athletes wait for the perfect wave, and then paddle to catch it. A panel of judges evaluate each ride to determine which surfer wins.

How the Sport Began

Riding the waves originated from Polynesians in Tahiti and Hawaii. Surfing was popularised by a native Hawaiian Olympic athlete, Duke Kahanamoku. Kahanamoku is considered 'the father of modern surfing' and planted the seed for its future Olympic inclusion; he expressed his dream to see the sport become an Olympic sport while accepting his medal at the 1912 Games.

Understanding the Sport

Competitors use "shortboards," smaller, performance-oriented surfboards that are designed for tight turns, vertical maneuvers, and top end speed on good waves. Each heat lasts 30 minutes. Surfers are allowed to catch as many waves as they can. Like gymnastics skills, each wave is given a difficulty from 1 - 5 and that combined with the surfers execution on a scale of 1 - 10 deteremines their score. The judge with the highest and lowest scores are tossed. The surfer's two highest scores are averaged for the overall heat score.

John John Florence

Track the Medals

Tokyo Olympic Qualifier

With help from his mother, John John first rode on a surfboard when he was six-months old, and he was surfing on his own by the age of five!

SURFING BROADCAST SCHEDULE

Medal Matches

7/28

Watch all of the action on the networks of NBCUniversal including

Fun Facts

In February 2020, Brazilian surfer Maya Gabeira surfed a wave that was 73.5 feet tall, breaking her own world record for largest wave surfed by a woman.

The first major surf contest was held in 1928 in California.

Duke Kahanamoku - known as the "father of surfing" - travelled the world with surfboards made of Hawaiian koa wood that weighed more than 100 pounds

Who's Competing?

Follow your favorite athletes.

NAME	SCORE

Scan me for more about Surfing!

Did You Know?

The surfing schedule is dependent on expected wave conditions. While the norm for some sports is to postpone competition in case of bad weather, surfing is known to postpone competition if better conditions are expected later.

Surfing

Word Search

S C G I G Z G Y J U U M A U Y
P H V M L V L F S G H R E B K
I B O V K E V Q I I Z U R J E
I Y H R Y Q W C M N N C I U P
Q L C L T G A C Q F S J A E Z
G F B R P B L G D M W M L G A
F R N W E E O M A X E J Q O W
V R O M J S X A E R L H B O A
I C S M H J T D R M L V R F M
K O U F J Q F Q H D N R A Y K
B P U T S K W P L R U M X F T
G M G H B X T N C H Y K E O I
K P O R J A W O A G V C D O A
L S R E P Q C X E H V Y R T N
C A R V I N G K W M U P M D L

AERIAL
AXED
CARVING
CREST
CUTBACK
FIN
GOOFYFOOT
GROM
SHORTBOARD
SWELL

Compare & Contrast

Compare and contrast the advantages of using a shortboard over a longboard in olympic competition.

Fact or Fiction

Circle the check mark if the statement is true, circle the 'x' if it is false.

1. The biggest wave ever recorded was 1738ft  
2. Cave paintings in France depict surfing over 20,000 years ago  

Discussion Questions

1. Surfers can ride up to 25 waves per round. What factors do you think play a part in their wave selection?
2. Each wave a surfer rides is judged on a variety of criteria. Which part of the wave do you think is the most challenging?
3. While the U.S. and Australia have been dominant in surfing, Brazil is breaking in as a strong contender. Why do you think that is?

Want to know more about Surfing?
Visit USA Surfing at www.usasurfing.org

Swimming

Swimming is an individual or team racing sport that requires the use of one's body to move through water (e.g., in a pool, sea, or lake). Competitive swimming is also an Olympic sport, with varied distance events in the butterfly, backstroke, breaststroke, freestyle, and individual medley.

How the Sport Began

Swimming is one of the world's oldest sports, with evidence of it being practiced in ancient Egypt, Greece, and Rome. Organized swimming competitions began on a regular basis in the 19th century. Four swimming events were included on the program at the first modern Olympic Games in Athens in 1896, and it's one of five sports that's been part of every Olympics — along with gymnastics, track and field, cycling, and fencing.

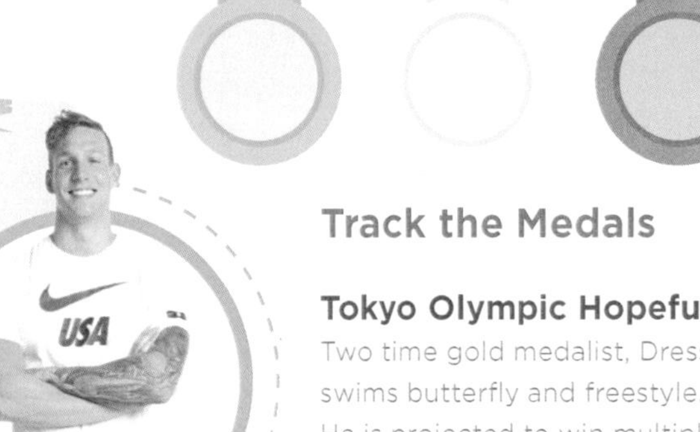

Understanding the Sport

The goal of competitive swimming is to break personal or world records while beating competitors in any given event.

The strokes allowed in competitive swimming are freestyle (crawl), backstroke, breaststroke, and butterfly — all four strokes are used in medley races.

Each stroke requires a set of specific swimming techniques; competitions have distinct regulations on acceptable forms for each one.

Caeleb Dressel

Track the Medals

Tokyo Olympic Hopeful

Two time gold medalist, Dressel swims butterfly and freestyle. He is projected to win multiple medals in Tokyo. Will he best Phelps' eight?

SWIMMING BROADCAST SCHEDULE

Men & Women

7/25 7/26 7/27 7/28 7/29 7/30 7/31 8/1

Mixed Team

7/31

Who's Competing?

Follow your favorite athletes.

NAME	TIME

Watch all of the action on the networks of NBCUniversal including

Scan me for more details about Swimming!

Fun Facts

Michael Phelps has been featured 3 times. He is so decorated they created a special 'Lifetime Achievement' box for his third appearance.

Swimming burns about 30% more calories per hour than running.

Breastroke is the oldest known swimming stroke.

Did You Know?

The crawl (freestyle) is the fastest Olympic swim stroke.

Compare & Contrast

Most sports—like swimming, soccer, tennis, and golf—are the same, regardless of whether the athletes are male or female. Use the space to the right to compare and contrast the two.

Crossword

DOWN

1 The time registered by a swimmer when he or she finishes each length of the pool

2 When swimmers somersault before reaching the wall and push off with their feet

5 The area at the edges of the pool into which water overflows during a race

6 To withdraw from an event in a competition

7 The gradual process of resting in preparation for competition

ACROSS

3 To move on the starting blocks prior to the starting signal

4 The area from which a swimmer dives into the pool to begin a race

8 The area at the end of each lane in the pool where a swimmer's time is registered

9 Refers to short intense swims of usually not more than 100 meters

10 Type of wave action caused by the bodies moving through the water

Want to know more about Swimming?
Visit USA Swimming at www.usaswimming.org

Table Tennis

Table tennis is one of the most popular sports in the world. It is played by two or four people on a table split in half by a short net. Player hit small plastic balls with rubber-coated paddles over the net to score points.

How the Sport Began

The first players used the lids of cigar boxes for rackets and a rounded-off wine corks over a row of books. Table tennis has also been known as 'ping pong,' 'whiff waff,' and 'flim flam,' which reflected the sound of striking the ball. Today, the game is played with paddles comprising of a wooden blade coated with rubber on both sides, and a hollow plastic ball weighing just 2.7 grams (a little less than an ounce).

Track the Medals

Wang Nan

Four Time Olympic Champion

One of only three ahletes to win four Olympic gold medals in table tennis.

TABLE TENNIS BROADCAST SCHEDULE

Men		Women		Mixed Team
7/30	8/6	7/29	8/5	7/26

Watch all of the action on the networks of NBCUniversal including

Understanding the Sport

A table is 9 feet long, 5 feet wide, 2.5 feet high, and divided by a net. This sport follows the same basic rules as tennis but has different scoring.

Singles matches are played over the best of 7 games. First player to 11 points (winning by 2) wins each game. Team matches consist of 4 singles matches and one doubles match, each played over the best of 5 games. Each team consists of 3 players and matches end when a team wins 3 individual games.

In Tokyo, there will be a mixed doubles event with one athlete of each gender on a team. Matches will be played to the best of 7 games, with each game played to 11 points (winning by 2).

Scan me for more!

Who's Competing?

Follow your favorite athletes.

NAME	WINS/LOSSES

Did You Know?

China has nearly three times as many Olympic medals in table tennis than any other country (53). The next best country, South Korea, has only 18.

Fun Facts

The longest table tennis match recorded in modern history lasted 1 hour, 32 minutes and 44 seconds!

Table tennis is the sixth largest sport in the world in terms of participation.

The first paddle believed to be used in table tennis was the back of a cigar box, and the first net was a stack of books. The first ball was a wine cork.

Table Tennis

Word Scramble

RKTCAAET ______________________

LKBCO ______________________

HPOC ______________________

NTLECOUOROP ______________________

GIPR ______________________

POOL ______________________

LPEOOR ______________________

EDPNHORLE GPRI ______________________

DSEKANHAH RPIG ______________________

PISTPON ______________________

Compare & Contrast

Compare and contrast the advantages and disadvantages between singles, doubles, and mixed doubles

____

____

Fact or Fiction

Circle the check mark if the statement is true, circle the 'x' if it is false.

1. The longest rally was 32,000 total hits. ✓ ✗

2. Table tennis is to ping-pong as Kleenex is to tissues.  

Discussion Questions

1. During a match, you might see player moving further and further away from the table to hit the ball. Why do you think that is?

2. Players sometimes hold the paddle in a way that makes it look like it's upside down. Do you think that helps them hit the ball? Why?

3. China has won nearly every gold medal since the sport entered the Olympics. What do you think makes them so dominant?

Taekwondo

In taekwondo, athletes compete in one-on-one matches in which they earn points for hand attacks and kicks that they land on their opponent. Competitors receive points based on the most challenging techniques, such as spinning kicks to the head, which score higher than basic hand attacks to the torso.

How the Sport Began

Martial arts have been practiced on the Korean peninsula for thousands of years, and during the early 20th century, taekwondo became the most popular form with the Korean people. The sport's exact origin is unknown.

Understanding the Sport

Taekwondo is believed to be a martial art of Korean origin, similar to karate in Japan. It utilizes hands and feet in order to attack or defend from an adversary in a one-on-one combat format.

Matches are fought on a matted area. Each match consists of 3 rounds lasting 2 minutes, with one-minute breaks between rounds. Athletes score points for each successful attack they make and the athlete with the most points at the end of the match wins.

Anastasija Zolotic

Track the Medals

Tokyo Olympic Qualifier

Silver medalist at the 2018 Buenos Aires Youth Olympic Games, Zolotic is ranked 7th in the world. At 5-foot-11 she's tall and strong, fights with an aggressive style and is looking for her first Olympic medal.

TAEKWONDO BROADCAST SCHEDULE

Men & Women

7/24 7/25 7/26 7/27

Watch all of the action on the networks of NBCUniversal including

Fun Facts

Often associated, taekwondo and karate differ in practice: taekwondo features more kicking than punching, while karate involves more punching than kicking.

Taekwondo incorporates a philosophy of living in the core teaching of the sport. Its five basic tenets are courtesy, integrity, perseverance, self-control, and indomitable spirit.

If there is a tie after the regulation period, there is a final sudden-death round known as the "golden point round."

Who's Competing?

Follow your favorite athletes.

NAME	SCORE

Scan for more about Taekwondo!

Did You Know?

Taekwondo levels are measured in belt colors, ranging from the white belt (beginner) to the black belt (master).

Taekwondo

Word Search

D X S T X K Y U B H J E O N F
T Y C T N F D J V D O J A N G
W J H S E M A E G W X F G O Q
G C A N H Z X U X E U Q F P H
M W R M O F H M X X Z G L Y C
Q B Y P G N R W X E K Z D T F
F C E S U K Y E O N G R Y E J
Z Z O K K B X O S Y I K A K V
I T T E U J X D C L Y I G K N
K X F S Q O C U Z Q Z A Z X W
K G Y O R O O G I W F K K U H
K E B X S S I T P O O M S A E
E Z Y V X I D X Y B N N W W B
H J I E Z M Q Q D O B O K J B
F E H X Y Y F H S M O K E U F

CHA-RYEOT
DOBOK
DOJANG
HOGU
GYOROOGI
JEON
JEUM
JOO SIM
KYEONG-RYE
POOMSAE

Compare & Contrast

Taekwondo matches take place on an octagonal field, while karate is on a square. What do you think are the advantages or disadvantages for each?

Athlete Bio

Who is your favorite athlete?

Describe their career & achievements.

NAME AGE COUNTRY

Discussion Questions

1. Competitors wear padded helmets to protect against kicks to the head. Can you think of other differences between taekwondo and karate?
2. Taekwondo competitors wear special uniforms that electronically assign points when they strike their opponents. Why don't other events use this technology?

Want to know more about Taekwondo?
Visit USA Taekwondo at www.teamusa.org/usa-taekwondo

Tennis

Tennis is a racket sport that can be played against a single opponent (singles), or between two teams of two players (doubles).

How the Sport Began

Tennis originated in France during the 12th century, when the first courts appeared in the courtyards of castles and monasteries. By the 13th century, there were close to 1,800 courts in France.

It was originally known as jeu de paume (the game of the palm) because players would hit a ball with their bare hands. Eventually a glove was used to protect the hand, and by the 14th century, the first rackets were used.

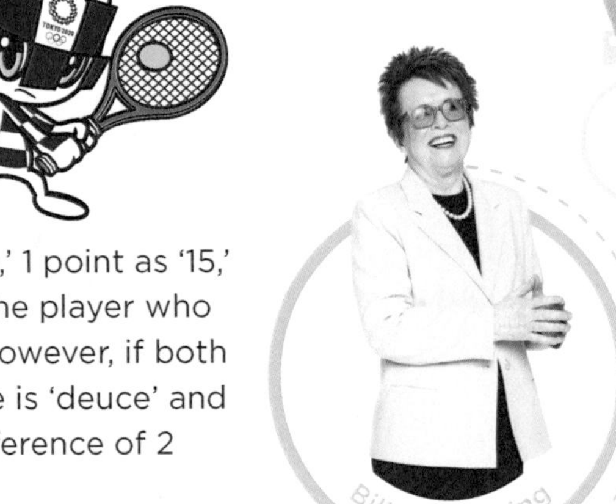

Track the Medals

Understanding the Sport

Tennis scoring counts 0 points as 'love,' 1 point as '15,' 2 points as '30,' and 3 points as '40.' The player who scores 4 points first wins that game. However, if both players have scored 3 points, the score is 'deuce' and the game continues until there is a difference of 2 points between the players.

The first player to win 6 games with a two-game advantage over their opponent wins the set.

At the Tokyo Games, the tournament will follow a knockout format for both men's and women's singles and doubles, as well as mixed doubles. Matches will be played on hard courts, which is the usual surface for the Olympic tournament.

Billie Jean King

Olympic Coach & Tennis Legend

Was part of the 'Battle of the Sexes' exhibition game. 90 million viewers watched. King beat Bobby Riggs.

Scan me for more!

TENNIS BROADCAST SCHEDULE

Men		Women		Mixed Team
7/30	8/1	7/31	8/1	8/1

Watch all of the action on the networks of NBCUniversal including

Who's Competing?

Follow your favorite athletes.

NAME	WINS/LOSSES

Did You Know?

Andy Murray of Great Britain is the only man to win two Olympic gold medals in singles.

Fun Facts

Venus & Serena Williams have four Olympic gold medals each. Each has won a singles gold and each have three doubles golds.

The first tennis balls were made of wool or hair wrapped in leather.

In 2010, Wimbledon has changed their rules of play after a single match lasted 11 hours and 5 minutes over 3 days.

Tokyo 2020

Tennis

Compare & Contrast

Compare and contrast the different advantages between singles, doubles, and mixed doubles events.

____

____

____

Crossword

6 SERVEANDVOLLEY

4 CHIPANDCHARGE

DOWN

1 When a player hits a groundstroke in attempt to pass an opponent who has taken position at the net

2 If both serve attempts fail. The opponent wins the point

3 If the server's foot enters the court before the service is completed

4 To hit a shot with backspin (slice) and follow it into the net

5 When a ball is hit just after it bounces

7 Occurs when a player hits the ball before it bounces

ACROSS

6 To follow a serve immediately into the net with the intent of winning the point with a volley or a forced error by the opponent

8 A valid serve that is not reached by the opponent

9 A tie game at 40 points

10 Zero points

Track & Field

Track and field (Athletics) is a sport which includes athletic contests of running, jumping, and throwing. Athletes are judged by the fastest time, the longest or highest jumps, and throws.

How the Sport Began

The roots of track and field can be traced back to the first ancient Olympic Games, held in 776 BCE, in the valley of Olympia on the southwestern coast of Greece.

The ancient Olympic Games were held every four years and eventually grew to contain other events, including the discus, javelin, and the broad jump.

Understanding the Sport

Most track and field events are individual sports with a single victor; the most prominent team events are relay races, which typically feature teams of four.

The foot-racing events include sprints (50 yards to 500 meters), middle-distance (800-2,000 meters), long-distance (3,000 to 30,000 meters), racewalking, and hurdling and are won by the athlete who completes it in the shortest time.

Field events include high jump, pole vault, long jump, triple jump, shot put, discus, javelin, and hammer. Jumping and throwing events are won by those who achieve the greatest distance or height.

Scan me for more!

Noah Lyles

Track the Medals

Tokyo Olympic Hopeful

In addition to his stellar athletic career, he is also a rapper and recording artist and can be found on Spotify under the handle Nojo18.

Who's Competing?

Follow your favorite athletes.

NAME	TIME/DISTANCE

TRACK & FIELD BROADCAST SCHEDULE

Men

7/31 8/1 8/2 8/3 8/4 8/5 8/6 8/7 8/8

Women

8/1 8/2 8/3 8/4 8/6 8/7

Mixed Team

8/1

Watch all of the action on the networks of NBCUniversal including

Fun Facts

In addition to gracing the front of a Wheaties box, Stacy Dragila has a street named after her on the Idaho State University campus.

The first Olympic race was in Greece in 776 BCE.

The Olympic 100-meter race determines who is the "fastest on earth."

Did You Know?

Over 200 countries participate in major track & field meets, including the Olympics.

Word Scramble

ABOTN ______

EDFIL VNTEE ______

LRUSEHD ______

NGOL IDCTANSE ______

LEOP VUTAL ______

NSPTRI ______

ETARSEDGG RSTTA ______

HIHG UPJM ______

Compare & Contrast

Compare and contrast the difference in track events versus field events.

Track & Field

Discussion Questions

1. Sprints and distance races have different demands on the body. What do each of these events require physically?
2. Of each of the track and field events, which events are you most excited for? Why?
3. When track events are marked, some lanes appear to be closer to the finish line than others. Why do you think that is?

Name the Events

Name 5 events that are part of Track & Field (athletics).

1. ______
2. ______
3. ______
4. ______
5. ______

USATF

Want to know more about Track & Field?
Visit USA Track & Field at www.usatf.org

Triathlon

The triathlon is an endurance sport that combines swimming, road cycling, and distance running, performed in that order. Events are conducted over a variety of distances but the Olympic distance for men and women is a 1,500-meter swim, 40-kilometer bike ride, and a 10-kilometer run.

How the Sport Began

The sport developed in the United States during the 1970s and became part of the Olympics at the 2000 Sydney Games. More than half a million spectators lined the city streets to cheer on the athletes.

Track the Medals

Understanding the Sport

The triathlon will feature the men's and women's race and a new mixed team relay event this year in Tokyo.

A triathlon race is completed without breaks from start to finish; both the men's and women's events consist of a single race and the first athlete to cross the finish line is the winner.

The new mixed team relay teams consists of 4 athletes (2 men, 2 women) who each complete a super-sprint triathlon (still a swim-bike-run, but shorter distance) before tagging the next person on their team. The team whose fourth competitor crosses the finish line first wins.

Scan me for more details about Triathlon!

Katie Zaferes

Tokyo Olympic Hopeful

Zaferes was a multisport athlete in high school. In college she ran track and won the state title for the 1500m. It wasn't until after college that she discovered her true passion.

Who's Competing?

Follow your favorite athletes.

NAME	TIME

TRIATHLON BROADCAST SCHEDULE

Men	Women	Mixed Team
7/26	7/27	7/31

Watch all of the action on the networks of NBCUniversal including

Did You Know?

The most well-known (and longest) version of the triathlon is the Ironman race. An Ironman consists of a 2.4-mile swim, a 112-mile bike and a 26.2-mile run. Top competitors can finish an Ironman in under nine hours.

Fun Facts

Hunter Kemper is the most decorated U.S. triathlete and a member of an elite group of athletes to be featured on the front of a Wheaties box.

It is not uncommon for triathletes to burn up to 10,000 calories during a race.

The oldest known triathlete is Arthur Gilbert, who was still competing at the age of 93!

Word Search

```
T R A N S I T I O N A R E A Q
F Y P D R A F T I N G X V L N
D N S V F C B F F H T K G I Z
E J O H Q D E W O R P Y N S E
M W A Y D J F D D A J B K I I
T Y W C V B A R O C B Y G N B
H A A L Y B V K K I Z T Z I U
Z W V I M R J D L N D Z P B T
S J E P J E S U R G E U J M M
K I S O R A C E P A C K E T R
Q T B N U K H T D G S W T U N
X U U S W A V D S E A O I X H
S R T P N W I S O Z A Z D Y L
E N G W G A Q R Y F M A D P S
Y V P R U Y V E V Z B Y E S A
```

BREAKAWAY
CLIP-ONS
DNS
DRAFTING
ITU
RACING AGE
RACE PACKET
SURGE
TRANSITION AREA
WAVES

Triathlon

Compare & Contrast

Compare and contrast each of the three events in the triathlon.

Discussion Questions

1. Triathletes must complete the event without any breaks. Which part do you think is the hardest, or the easiest? Why?
2. The sport has always started with swimming and ended with a run. Why do you think that is?

Picture Math

Can you solve the equation?

+ + = 24

+ + = 19

+ + = 15

+ x = __

Volleyball

Volleyball is a team sport of six players on each side, separated by a large net. They hit a soft ball over the net to try and score points against the opposing team.

How the Sport Began

The sport was first introduced as 'mintonette' in 1895 by William G. Morgan for members of his YMCA gym in Massachusetts.

Volleyball spread globally when the International Volleyball Federation (FIVB) was established in 1947. The first men's World Championship took place the following year, while the first World Championship for women was held in 1952.

Understanding the Sport

Volleyball matches are played to the best of 5 sets. Each set is played to 25 points with a team needing a two-point advantage to win. When a team wins a point they serve next. The first team to 3 sets wins the match, but when the match is tied at 2 sets each, the final set is played to 15 points.

At the upcoming Tokyo Olympics, teams will be divided into two pools of six, with each pool playing a round robin. The top four teams of each pool advance to the quarterfinals; the final round is played under a knock-out system.

Track the Medals

Three Time Olympic Champion

Won Olympic gold in beach and indoor volleyball. He also coached the women's team in Rio leading them to Bronze.

VOLLEYBALL BROADCAST SCHEDULE

Men	Women
8/7	8/8

Watch all of the action on the networks of NBCUniversal including

Fun Facts

The longest volleyball game lasted 85 hours!

The first ball to be specially designed for volleyball was created in 1896.

Volleyball was originally an indoor-only game. Beach volleyball started in the 1920s in California.

Who's Competing?

Follow your favorite athletes.

NAME	POSITION

Scan for more about Volleyball!

Did You Know?

Around 800 million people worldwide play volleyball in a week.

Compare & Contrast

Research and list 6 differences between court and beach volleyball.

1. ______________________
2. ______________________
3. ______________________
4. ______________________
5. ______________________
6. ______________________

Crossword

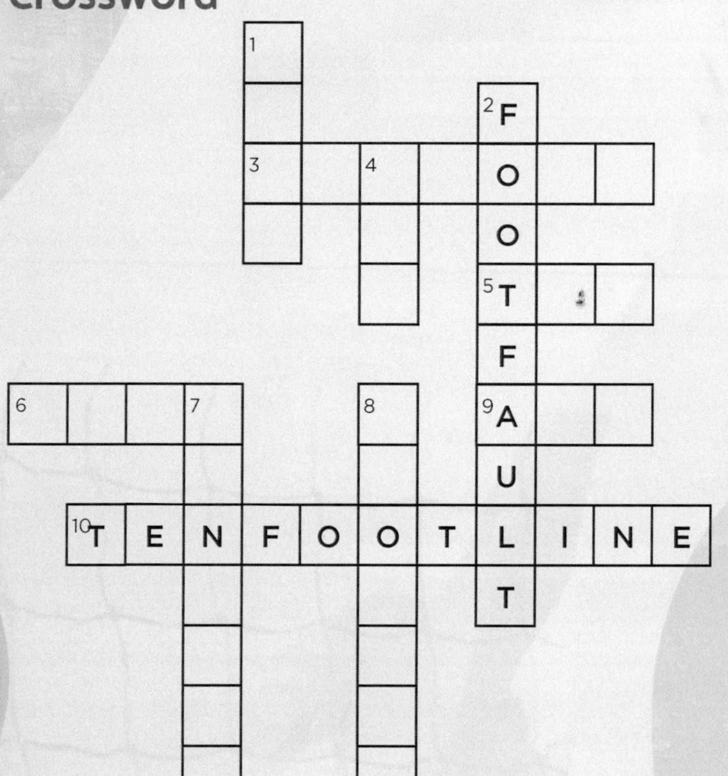

DOWN

1 A technique used to receive the opponent's hit and pass the ball to a fellow teammate

2 When the server steps on or across the back line before serving the ball.

4 To prevent a hard-hit attack from hitting the ground by passing it up with any part of the body.

7 A player puts his or her hand flat on the floor and lets the ball bounce off the back of it to prevent the ball from hitting the floor.

8 A serve with no spin that wobbles through the air like a knuckleball in baseball.

ACROSS

3 When the team that received the serve wins the point and is awarded the next serve.

5 A ball hit softly over the net, instead of attacking.

6 When the setter sends the ball over the net on the second hit instead of setting it to a hitter.

9 A serve that lands in bounds and goes unplayed by the opposing team, resulting in a point for the serving team.

10 The line that marks 10 feet from the net.

Water Polo

Water polo is a competitive, full-contact team sport. Teams have six players and a goalie with the objective to score more goals than the opposing team.

Because the water polo ball resembles a volleyball, many people assume water polo is just volleyball in the water. It's actually much more closely related to rugby or soccer.

How the Sport Began

In 1869, an English rowing club set out to create a game similar to soccer, but in the water. They came up with "football in water," which would later be known as water polo.

WATER POLO BROADCAST SCHEDULE

Men	Women

8/8	8/7

Watch all of the action on the networks of NBCUniversal including

Understanding the Sport

For water polo, teams of 7 tread water or swim the entire game and cannot touch the bottom or sides of the pool. Except for the goalie, players may only handle the ball with one hand. The object is to put the ball into the opponent's net. Physical contact is also highly encouraged. Water polo is unique in that other than the five-meter penalty throws, the whistle does not stop play.

Men's and women's water polo rules are nearly identical. Upon taking control of the ball, the offensive team has 30 seconds to shoot, or it loses possession. A shot clock at each end of the pool helps the players keep track.

Track the Medals

Rio Olympic Gold Medalist

Steffens comes from a family of water polo players. Her father Carlos, uncle Peter Carlos, uncle Peter and three siblings all played. Her older sister won a silver medal at the London Games.

Did You Know?

Men play with a slightly larger ball and on a field that is 16 feet longer than the women. Otherwise the rules are virtually the same.

Fun Facts

Along with soccer, water polo was the first team sport to be included in the Olympics.

The average player swims nearly two miles in a game.

Olympic water polo players can throw the ball up to 50 miles per hour.

Water Polo

Word Scramble

BNYUN OSHT ______________________

LIATBRYUT ______________________

DRY SSAP ______________________

ENEIEGR ______________________

ETBAEGERG ______________________

INGBIRLBD ______________________

RDE ARDC ______________________

IGLANTLS ______________________

WET SAPS ______________________

WGNI ______________________

Fact or Fiction

Circle the check mark if the statement is true, circle the 'x' if it is false.

1. Added with tug-of-war to the 1900 Olympic Games.  
2. Until 1950, players pedaled around in the water on mechanical horses.  

Compare & Contrast

Water polo is similar to handball, except that it's played in a pool. Can you think of other similarities or differences?

____

____

____

____

____

____

____

Discussion Questions

1. European countries have been strong contenders, with Hungary winning the most gold medals. Why do you think that is?
2. Teams only get 30 seconds to pass to their teammates and score. Can you think of other sports with time limits before they lose possession?
3. The men's competition started in 1900, but women's didn't join until 2000. Why do you think that is?
4. Water polo is the only ball sport played in a pool. Can you think of other sports that would be fun to play in a pool?

Weightlifting

Weightlifting is a sport in which athletes lift barbells from the ground to above their heads, competing to lift the greatest amount of weight.

How the Sport Began

Weightlifting dates back to ancient Egypt and Greece, and continued through the Middle Ages, usually done by the strongest men in villages all over Europe. In the 1800s, professionals toured with carnivals or vaudeville shows. By the end of the 19th century, weightlifting was recognized as a competitive sport internationally. It was included in the first modern Olympic Games in 1896.

WEIGHTLIFTING BROADCAST SCHEDULE

Men

7/25	7/28	7/31	8/3	8/4

Women

7/24	7/26	7/27	8/1	8/2

Watch all of the action on the networks of NBCUniversal including

Understanding the Sport

Weightlifting athletes are divided into weight classes. Each athlete has 3 attempts at both the snatch (lifting the bar from their feet to above their head in a squat position, then pushing up to a standing position) and the clean and jerk (lifting the bar from the floor to rest on their chest with bent arms [the clean] and then using a jumping motion to extend both the arms and legs to stand upright with the weight fully extended overhead [the jerk]).

An athlete's best snatch is added to their best clean and jerk to calculate the total amount of weight lifted, and the athlete with the highest total weight wins.

Jourdan Delacruz

Track the Medals

Tokyo Olympic Qualifier

At just five feet tall, Jourdan Delacruz is the smallest member of Team USA Weightlifting.

Who's Competing?

Follow your favorite athletes.

NAME	WEIGHT

Scan for more information about Weightlifting!

Did You Know?

In 1928, the program was standardized to three lifts: snatch, clean & jerk, and press. In 1976, the press was removed because of judging difficulty.

Fun Facts

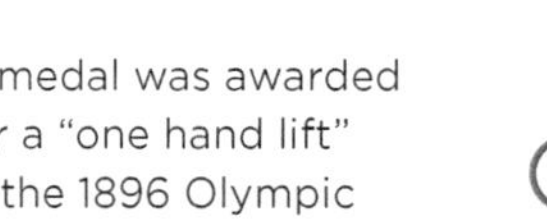

A medal was awarded for a "one hand lift" in the 1896 Olympic games before the event was discontinued.

Weightlifting has been on the program of every modern Olympic Games except in 1900, 1908, and 1912.

Athletes choose the weight for their first attempt; it can only get heavier. A lifter starting too high might face trouble.

Weightlifting

Word Search

```
H H V H P U M G L Q I E O C C
P R D C L E A N A N D J E R K
L T V O X X H B F H G P K C B
A Q L P M X W O X K S I S S B
T A B K C N U N N G Q V P K T
E O F I M M B S T K U T L X N
S P G R J M I P T K A B I O O
V L P R E S S O U T T S T I L
A D N H K Q B Z C V G N W S I
A T T E M P T O P K S A X L F
D A M S J M P K M U A T T H T
H M Y X T E A B O B F C W C D
O A Y A U R H C K L O H P H T
D H O O K I N G F F T U Z W F
Y V X Z N E P J A U N H T A L
```

ATTEMPT
BOMB-OUT
CLEAN AND JERK
HOOKING
NO LIFT
PLATES
PRESS OUT
SNATCH
SPLIT
SQUAT

Compare & Contrast

Compare and contrast the different events for weightlifting.

____

____

____

____

Order of Elements

Number the parts of the clean & jerk lifts in the correct order.

 ________

 ________

 ________

 ________

 ________

 ________

Discussion Questions

1. Weightlifters are split into 10 weight classes for the 2021 Olympics. What advantages to lighter weight classes have over heavier classes, and vice versa?

2. While strength is required, it also requires mental focus. What techniques would you use to maintain focus if you were competing?

Wrestling

Wrestling is a competition in which two athletes (wrestlers) try to pin the each other to the mat. Striking is not allowed, but wrestlers can use throws and takedowns to get their opponent down to the ground.

How the Sport Began

Wrestling was a feature of the ancient Olympic Games in 708 BCE. The sport's Greco-Roman style was included in the first modern Olympic Games in 1896. Eight years later, freestyle wrestling was introduced at the 1904 St. Louis Games. Women's freestyle wrestling joined the Olympic program in 2004.

Track the Medals

WRESTLING BROADCAST SCHEDULE

Men & Women

8/2 8/3 8/4 8/5 8/6 8/7

Watch all of the action on the networks of NBCUniversal including

Understanding the Sport

Wrestling matches are contested on a circular mat that's 12 meters in diameter. Matches last for two periods of three minutes with a 30-second break. Athletes earn points for a variety of actions and holds, including forcing an opponent out of bounds, taking an opponent down, and rolling an opponent into an exposed position. At the end of both periods, the athlete with most points wins.

There are two wrestling styles. The chief difference is that in Greco-Roman, a wrestler may not attack below the waist or use his own legs to trip, lift, or execute other holds. In freestyle, both the arms and legs are used to execute holds.

Tokyo Olympic Qualifier

Gray designed a special edition shoe for ASICS. The Aggressor 3 L.E. Adeline Gray wrestling shoe is the first for a female wrestler.

Who's Competing?

Follow your favorite athletes.

NAME	WINS/LOSSES

Scan for more information about Wrestling!

Did You Know?

Wrestling was part of the ancient Olympics since the 18th Olympiad in 708 B.C. It first appeared as an elimination tournament among the Greeks and was the decisive discipline of the Ancient Games Pentathlon.

Fun Facts

Since 1994, the number of U.S. girls' high school wrestlers has increased from 804 to over 20,000.

The U.S. has won 133 medals in wrestling at the Olympics, the most of any nation.

Wrestling is often considered the oldest sport on Earth. Cave drawings that depict the sport date back to 3,000 BCE.

Ways to Win

Name the three ways you can win in a wrestling bout.

1. ______________________ 2. ______________________ 3. ______________________

Wrestling

Crossword

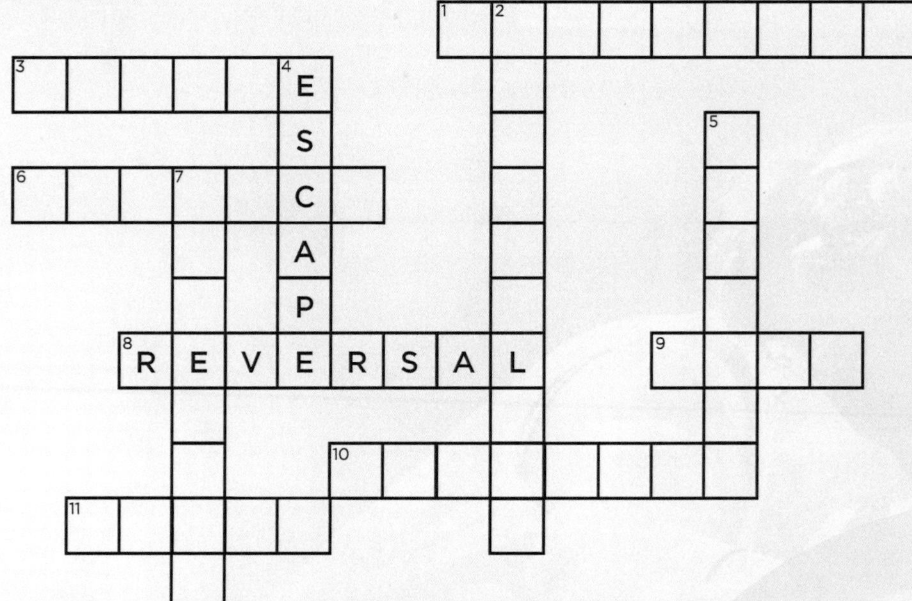

DOWN

2 When a wrestler passes his or her arm under his or her opponent's armpit from behind and places the palm of his or her hand against the back of the head.

4 When the wrestler on the bottom manages to get to his or her feet and face their opponent.

5 Also known as an ankle lace.

7 When a wrestler takes his or her opponent to the mat from a standing position.

ACROSS

1 A 30-second period where one wrestler who has been designated as passive is required to score a point.

3 A defensive move in which a wrestler, while facing belly-up, attempts to avoid being pinned by supporting himself or herself with his or her head and feet.

6 When the referee orders a wrestler to place both hands on the back of his or her opponent, who is underneath on the ground.

8 When the wrestler on the bottom reverses positions with the wrestler on top and seizes control.

9 Called when both shoulders of the defensive wrestler are held against the mat for the length of time it takes the referee to pronounce the word "tombe," about half a second.

10 When a wrestler turns his or her opponent's shoulders to the mat.

11 When the referee encourages wrestlers to be more active.

Want to know more about Wrestling?
Visit USA Wrestling at www.teamusa.org/usa-wrestling

answer guide

Answer Guide

The Ancient Games - Page 2

1. 776 BCE
2. All free Greek males were allowed to take part, from farmhands to royal heirs, although the majority of Olympians were soldiers. And while there is some evidence that women participated in the early Games, by the fifth century BCE, women were explicitly barred from competition and the Games as a whole.
3. A wreath of olives as this was associated with Heracles, a demi-god associated with the Olympic Games.
4. Twelve centuries

The Modern Games - Page 4

1. **The first meeting of the International Olympic Committee (IOC) was held in** Sorbonne in Paris, France **in** 1894.
2. **Women were officially allowed to compete starting in the** 1900 **Olympic Games.**
3. **The first modern Olympic Games was held in** Athens, Greece **in** 1896.

Archery - Page 22

For all archery puzzle solutions, go to: sportsengine.com/archery-puzzles.pdf

1. There are many reasons why the use of the bow and arrow declined with the invention of firearms. One reason is that guns, if aimed correctly, can be more accurate than a bow and arrow. Guns are also more powerful, and can be used quicker.
2. The different size circles and colors on the targets are used to test accuracy. Some circles are harder to hit than others.
3. The feathers at the end of arrows are used to stabilize the arrows as they fly through the air. This makes each shot more accurate.

Artistic Swimming - Page 24

For all artistic swimming puzzle solutions, go to: sportsengine.com/artistic-swimming-puzzles.pdf

1. Artistic swimming is scored by a panel of judges. In order for the judges to determine who has the best technique for a certain skill, they need to see all teams showcase that same skill. Having a designated set of movements allows the judges to assess who has the best technique.

Badminton - Page 26

For all badminton puzzle solutions, go to: sportsengine.com/badminton-puzzles.pdf

1. Players serve first on the right side with a starting score of 0-0. That means when the server switches to the left side, the score will be 1-0, an odd number. When the server switches back to the right, the score will either be 1-1 or 2-0, which means the total score is an even 2. The game continues like that, with odd scores on the left and evens on the right. It's a good way to make sure the score is right!
2. A shuttlecock has feathers to keep it from wobbling in the air during play. The feathers allow the shuttlecock to change speed and direction very rapidly without being wobbly or losing speed.

Baseball - Page 28

For all baseball puzzle solutions, go to: sportsengine.com/baseball-puzzles.pdf

1. Japan recognized how popular baseball is all over the world. The country thought it was important to include a sport that is loved by all in the worldwide Olympic Games.

Basketball - Page 30

For all basketball puzzle solutions, go to: sportsengine.com/basketball-puzzles.pdf

1. The team included NBA greats like Larry Bird, Michael Jordan, and Magic Johnson. During the 1992 Barcelona Olympic Games, the team won by an average of 44 points over their competitors.

Beach Volleyball - Page 32

For all beach volleyball puzzle solutions, go to: sportsengine.com/beach-volleyball-puzzles.pdf

1. Indoor volleyball is played with six players to a side, while beach volleyball is only played with two players to a side. The indoor court is larger because twelve total players can cover more of the court during play, whereas a beach volleyball court is smaller because four total players cannot cover the same amount of court. Similarly, an indoor volleyball court is smaller because it allows for players to hit the ball harder and with greater speed, which can make for a faster play of game. Beach volleyballs are larger and lighter so that players have greater control over the ball.
2. Beach volleyball players need to know every skill because they don't have set positions on the court and they move constantly throughout play. Players could be put in a position to hit, block, or dig at any time during a game, and so they must be prepared for any type of scenario.

Boxing - Page 34

For all boxing puzzle solutions, go to: sportsengine.com/boxing-puzzles.pdf

1. Olympic competitors wear padded helmets to increase the safety of the athletes. This is especially important because Olympic boxers must compete in many matches in a short period of time.
2. There are many reasons why lighter and heavier weight classes have different approaches to boxing. One reason is that lighter and heavier boxers have different centers of gravity, which affects how they throw punches and aim at an opponent.

Canoe - Page 36

For all canoe puzzle solutions, go to: sportsengine.com/canoe-puzzles.pdf

1. There are many different advantages and disadvantages to the types of paddles used by canoers and kayakers. One advantage of a kayaker's double blade is that it is easier to change direction since the kayaker does not have to switch the side of the boat he or she is paddling on. One advantage of a canoer's paddle might be that he or she has the ability to make longer strokes to move the boat farther.
2. Canoes have a longer, more slender shape while kayaks are a bit wider to account for a kayaker's in-boat seat. Due to its shape, a canoe might have a tougher time changing direction quickly, which means it would be more challenging in a slalom race.
3. Olympic slalom courses are often artificial in order to ensure fairness. Man-made courses allow for all athletes to be subjected to the same challenges during a race, which might not be guaranteed in open water.

Cycling - Page 38

For all cycling puzzle solutions, go to: sportsengine.com/cycling-puzzles.pdf

1. There are many tricks in BMX freestyle. Some include bunny hop, manual, 180, and bar hop.
2. There are many differences between the four different types of bicycles: BMX, Road, Mountain, and Track. BMX bikes are the smallest bike you'll see at the Olympics, with a very small, light frame, a single speed, and a free back wheel so riders can pedal backward while still moving. Road bikes have very light, strong frames with standard brakes and 22 different gear options. Mountain bikes have very wide and knobby tires that help to grip and navigate tough terrain, and they have 30 different gear options. Track bikes only have the essentials, such as one gear and no breaks.
3. European countries have a strong culture of cycling. It is not uncommon to see Europeans biking to work or the grocery store, or forgoing a car altogether. That daily culture can be seen translating to the massive success of European cycling teams in road and track races.

Diving - Page 40

For all diving puzzle solutions, go to: sportsengine.com/diving-puzzles.pdf

1. Diving uses many of the same techniques as gymnastics or dance. Divers do flips and turns that are similar to those in gymnastics routines. Divers also share similar body positioning and polishing that you find in dance, such as pointed toes.
2. The tighter a diver holds to their legs in a tuck, the faster their body can rotate. This becomes advantageous when divers do multiple somersaults in a row; faster somersaults mean more rotations and more time to come out of the tuck to land in the water.

Equestrian - Page 42

For all equestrian puzzle solutions, go to: sportsengine.com/equestrian-puzzles.pdf

1. Eventing consists of three main disciplines: dressage, cross-country, and jumping, and each are challenging in their own ways. Dressage requires the horse to be skillful and attentive to the rider while cross-country is a test of endurance. Jumping is difficult because it often occurs as the last event when the horse is already tired from the previous disciplines.
2. German-bred horses, such as the Trakehner, are typically outstanding in eventing. The Germans are very successful and devote a lot of resources to breeding competition horses.

Fencing - Page 44

For all fencing puzzle solutions, go to: sportsengine.com/fencing-puzzles.pdf

1. There are three types of swords in fencing: foil, epee, and sabre, each with a unique strategy behind it. To gain points using a foil, the fencer must be precise about where the point lands on their opponent. The epee favors fencers who are more patient, defensive, and thoughtful, while the sabre is all about the offensive attack.
2. There are advantages to using both speed and height. Height can allow a fencer to strike from a further distance since they have longer arms. Speed, on the other hand, can catch an opponent off guard and control the pace of the match.
3. Epee does not use the rule of priority, or right-of-way because of its dueling history! Traditionally, whoever lands the first touch wins the point, no matter who was attacking first.

Field Hockey - Page 46

For all field hockey puzzle solutions, go to: sportsengine.com/field-hockey-puzzles.pdf

1. There are many advantages to playing on artificial turf. For instance, there is less maintenance needed for artificial turf upkeep. Artificial turf also allows for a more fast-paced game.
2. Field hockey was played as early as the 14th century in England but gained rapid popularity in India, a British colony, in the 1800s. India was home to the very first professional field hockey team established outside of England, Calcutta HC, and the country went on to dominate competitions, including the Olympics. While predominantly a women's sport played in colleges in countries like the United States, field hockey is rapidly gaining popularity at the professional level, leading to more successes for countries outside of India.

Golf - Page 48

For all golf puzzle solutions, go to: sportsengine.com/golf-puzzles.pdf

Gymnastics - Page 50

For all gymnastics puzzle solutions, go to: sportsengine.com/gymnastics-puzzles.pdf

1. Gymnastics floors have built-in springs or a combination of rubber foam and plywood that make the entire floor bouncy.
2. The bell is a timer that allows the gymnast to know how much time he or she has left in their routine. Often there will be a bell to signal there are 10 seconds left in an athlete's allotted time.
3. The chalk helps the athletes grip the pommel horse, rings, or bars. It prevents the possibility of the athletes slipping off or losing their grip during the routine. This not only helps the gymnast's routine but can also enhance the safety of the athlete.
4. The line in the middle of the landing area is used as a guide to judge how straight a gymnast's jump was. The closer to that line the athlete lands, the more accurate the jump, and the better their score.
5. Each position, or "strength," in the rings must be held for a minimum of two seconds. The rings showcase upper-body skills: biceps, triceps, shoulders, and chest are the main muscles used in the rings.

Handball - Page 52

For all handball puzzle solutions, go to: sportsengine.com/handball-puzzles.pdf

1. In handball, athletes are allowed to not only throw to move the ball but dribble as well, like in basketball. An indoor court allows for easier dribbling, and it also speeds up the play of the game.
2. Referees can issue a "passive play" penalty if they don't see the offensive team actively trying to score. This keeps the game moving, but may pose an issue to teams trying to stick to a certain formation or strategic approach.
3. While it may seem more difficult to aim and shoot with your feet, handball has rules in place that state players can only shoot from a certain distance, making it harder to aim accurately and score past a goalkeeper in a smaller net.

Judo - Page 54

For all judo puzzle solutions, go to: sportsengine.com/judo-puzzles.pdf

1. Many forms of martial arts focus on pinning down an opponent. Another example is jiu-jitsu.
2. Judo is the fourth most popular sport in France, and many parents enroll their kids in the sport at a young age. The French people have deeply connected with the values of judo and the sport has become less of a recreational activity and more of a lifestyle education.

Karate - Page 56

For all karate puzzle solutions, go to: sportsengine.com/karate-puzzles.pdf

1. There are two main disciplines within Karate: Kumite and Kata. Kumite focuses on fighting techniques, like kicking and punching, while Kata is more about performance and demonstrating skill.
2. Each point system is challenging in its own way. Fencing, for example, takes into account the priority rule, Kumite allows for points based on the technique displayed, and boxing is scored by a judging panel.

Modern Pentathlon - Page 58

For all modern pentathlon puzzle solutions, go to: sportsengine.com/modern-pentathlon-puzzles.pdf

1. Each of the five events that comprise modern pentathlon aligns closely with skills needed to be successful on the battlefield. Running, swimming, shooting, horseback riding, and sword fighting are all traditional situations a military officer would be subjected to in the line of duty (at least up until WWII).
2. Each event could be challenging in its own way. Running and swimming pose a challenge because they require a lot of endurance. Show jumping or shooting, however, require a lot of specific techniques. Athletes must master a very wide range of skills in order to compete in modern pentathlon.

Rowing - Page 60
For all rowing puzzle solutions, go to: sportsengine.com/rowing-puzzles.pdf

Rugby - Page 62
For all rugby puzzle solutions, go to: sportsengine.com/rugby-puzzles.pdf

1. There are many aspects of soccer and American football that appear in rugby. Touchdown scoring and the huddle that starts play called the "scrum," are used similarly in American football. The way players move the ball down the field with consistent forward passing is similar to soccer.
2. Rugby players are taught to hit in a very specific way. They often lower their bodies to the level of their opponent's hips and assume a low crouch that allows them to lean their full force into the opponent. There is much less head-to-head contact in rugby than in American football, which accounts for fewer injuries.
3. After the 1924 Olympics, a new President of the IOC took office and wasn't very fond of the sport of rugby. He removed it from the Olympic program, along with some other team-based sports.

Sailing - Page 64
For all sailing puzzle solutions, go to: sportsengine.com/sailing-puzzles.pdf

1. In individual sailing events, individual boats compete against one another for first place. In team events, teams of three boats each compete against each other for the best overall finish. An advantage to competing as a team is that all boats have the ability to work together to better their chances of winning. One boat could help block the wind from another or help navigate a turn. An advantage to the individual race, however, is that an individual boat does not have to worry about what place other team members will finish in. An individual boat just has to worry about winning!er their body can rotate. This becomes advantageous when divers do multiple somersaults in a row; faster somersaults mean more rotations and more time to come out of the tuck to land in the water.
2. Sailing races are triangular in order to test different skills. Sailing in a triangle forces the sailor to execute complicated turns and navigate challenging changes in the wind.

Shooting - Page 66
For all shooting puzzle solutions, go to: sportsengine.com/shooting-puzzles.pdf

Skateboarding - Page 68
For all skateboarding puzzle solutions, go to: sportsengine.com/skateboarding-puzzles.pdf

1. There are a ton of different skateboarding tricks that can be performed, ranging in difficulty. Judges will score each trick on a scale of 0 - 100.0. A simple trick, like a kickflip, might not be worth a lot of points, but something extremely difficult like a gazelle flip might be worth close to the maximum 100.0 points.
2. Park and street events share a lot of the same basic tricks. Skateboarders would have to master simple jumps and lands, like an Ollie or a 360 flip. Both types of competition also use tricks like balancing, grinds, and slides.

Soccer - Page 70
For all soccer puzzle solutions, go to: sportsengine.com/soccer-puzzles.pdf

1. Soccer players are not only great athletes, they're often great actors as well. Many coaches encourage their players to "flop" or fall in order to force a penalty on the opposing team and get an advantage. While the faking may seem unfair at times, it has become such a staple in soccer that the dramatics are just another part of the game.

Softball - Page 72
For all softball puzzle solutions, go to: sportsengine.com/softball-puzzles.pdf

1. Softballs are larger and therefore do not travel as far or as fast as baseballs. While that may seem like an advantage, the pitcher's mound in softball is also closer to the plate, which means that the batter has less time to react to the throw. One advantage, however, is that softballs are yellow which makes them a bit easier to see as they're thrown.
2. A windmill-style pitch is much less harsh on the shoulder joint than an overhand pitch. Softball pitchers can often pitch for longer without sustaining injury, both in individual games and throughout their overall careers.
3. Similar to baseball, Japan has brought back softball for the 2020 Olympics because of the country's love of the sport. With that inspiration behind the Japanese national team, a repeat victory wouldn't be out of the question!

Sport Climbing - Page 74
For all sport climbing puzzle solutions, go to: sportsengine.com/sport-climbing-puzzles.pdf

1. Sport climbing has three main disciplines: speed, bouldering, and lead. Speed climbing is high-intensity and closest to a race format, while bouldering puts a climber's skill to the test. Lead tests how high a climber can go in a certain amount of time.
2. There are many different advantages and disadvantages to using safety ropes. One clear advantage is the added safety measure for the climber: if anything were to go wrong, the climber would be backed up by the ropes. One disadvantage could be how the ropes affect the mentality of the climber; some climbers might feel more capable if they weren't attached to anything at all.

Surfing - Page 76

For all surfing puzzle solutions, go to: sportsengine.com/surfing-puzzles.pdf

1. Part of being a good surfer is picking out the perfect wave. Choosing a wave is a skill in itself, and it is essential to being successful in competition. Surfers take a lot of factors into account when selecting a wave, such as the wind speed and direction, which way the wave is swelling, and how long of a period there is between waves. Surfers also try to look for the peak of the wave and identify how it breaks.
2. Judging takes into account a lot of different factors, from the height of a wave to the number of maneuvers completed by the surfer while riding the wave. Some may think choosing the right wave is the hardest part, while others might find the addition of tricks to be more challenging.
3. Brazil's rise in surfing competitions has been very recent. A large part of surfing's popularity in Brazil has to do with the near-perfect surfing conditions in the country. Brazil has some of the best surfing in the world, making it easy for Brazilians to master the sport.

Swimming - Page 78

For all swimming puzzle solutions, go to: sportsengine.com/swimming-puzzles.pdf

Table Tennis - Page 80

For all table tennis puzzle solutions, go to: sportsengine.com/table-tennis-puzzles.pdf

1. The ideal positioning in table tennis is to stand about an arms' length back from the table. Often players will move even further back as a rally progresses in order to better return balls. Standing further back allows for a player to better attack a long ball, and they are in a better position to step in to attack a short ball.
2. Players that hold that paddle "upside-down" are using a type of grip called a penhold. This type of grip has many advantages, including increased flexibility of the wrist, which allows players to hit better backhands and put a lot of spin on the ball.
3. Table tennis was declared the national sport of China in the 1950s. Its appeal was largely due to the fact that the sport doesn't call for a large space, such as a field or stadium, and it was a sport not quite popular in the West at the time. There are table tennis tables in most park spaces throughout the country, and a significant amount of the Chinese population plays the game, recreationally and professionally. Chinese professionals go through very rigorous training to rise to their dominant level.

Taekwondo - Page 82

For all taekwondo puzzle solutions, go to: sportsengine.com/taekwondo-puzzles.pdf

1. Unlike karate, taekwondo focuses on kicking as its main form of attack. Taekwando uses the hands as a backup to kicking, whereas karate uses kicking as a backup to throwing punches, therefore, each type uses a very different stance as well. Karate puts more emphasis on strength and power, while taekwondo praises flexibility, mobility, and speed.
2. Taekwondo uniforms include special sensors that detect when a fighter has been struck with a kick or punch by their opponent. This helps to score the overall match, as the athlete with the most points scored at the end is the winner. Other sports may not have the same rules and regulations as taekwondo that would allow for them to use this scoring. For example, fencing uses the priority rule to help determine who has landed a hit on their opponent, rather than just limiting points to who has struck first.

Tennis - Page 84

For all tennis puzzle solutions, go to: sportsengine.com/tennis-puzzles.pdf

Track & Field - Page 86

For all track & field puzzle solutions, go to: sportsengine.com/track-field-puzzles.pdf

1. Sprint and distance running use different physical techniques. Sprints are considered to be anaerobic events while distance races are aerobic, which means there are differences in how the body uses oxygen in each type of race. Sprints also use different types of muscles, called fast-twitch muscles, while distance running focuses on slow-twitch muscle movements.
2. There are many exciting events to keep an eye out for: hurdles and javelin are just a couple!
3. Because of the shape of a track, the outer lanes actually cover more distance per single lap, which means if you are running in an outer lane, you are running farther than an athlete in an inner lane. In order to make the races the same distance, the outer lanes are staggered. That's why it looks like some runners are getting a head start!

Triathlon - Page 88

For all triathlon puzzle solutions, go to: sportsengine.com/triathlon-puzzles.pdf

1. Think about the order of events: biking or running may seem easier than swimming in open water, but by the time an athlete gets to biking or running, they're already very tired!
2. The triathlon starts with the most potentially exhausting event first: swimming. This is for the athletes' safety so they don't get injured or too fatigued while finishing the race in open water.

Volleyball - Page 90

For all volleyball puzzle solutions, go to: sportsengine.com/volleyball-puzzles.pdf

Water Polo - Page 92

For all water polo puzzle solutions, go to: sportsengine.com/water-polo-puzzles.pdf

1. Europeans have been playing water polo since the 19th century, with the first water polo match hosted in London in 1870. After official rules were established, the game resembling "water rugby" spread across Europe in the late 1800s, before first landing in the United States in 1888.
2. Basketball is another sport that has a time limit before a team loses possession. The shot clock is most commonly 24 seconds.
3. Women were fighting to be included in the water polo event for over 20 years before they were allowed by the IOC. They held many protests to get their event on the Olympic schedule, but they were turned down each Games until Sydney 2000, when the Australian national team took home the gold medal. It was a massive victory for the home team and for women everywhere! Water polo is yet another event that has been subjected to gender inequality throughout Olympic history, and women have had to fight hard to have their sports recognized.
4. Think about playing basketball or volleyball in the pool!

Weightlifting - Page 94

For all weightlifting puzzle solutions, go to: sportsengine.com/weightlifting-puzzles.pdf

1. Size is very important in wrestling. It is not uncommon to see wrestlers change weight classes between big competitions. Often, wrestlers will try to strategize which weight class they will most likely dominate in. A wrestler may weigh enough and be strong enough to compete in a heavier weight class, but he or she might try to cut down their weight so that their superior strength can carry them to victory in a lighter weight class.
2. Athletes use a lot of techniques to maintain their focus. Some may meditate before a match, visualizing their opponent and playing out different scenarios in their heads. Some may focus on their breathing and try to remain calm while competing.

Wrestling - Page 96

For all wrestling puzzle solutions, go to: sportsengine.com/wrestling-puzzles.pdf

photo credits

Photocredits

Page 1

Unknown (2020) **Olympic flame handed over to Japan** [Photograph]. Kyodo News Stills via Getty Images. https://www.gettyimages.com/detail/1207648467
Unknown (1830) **Boxers in ancient Olympic Games** [Photograph]. Universal Images Group Editorial via Getty Images. https://www.gettyimages.com/detail/926723110
Unknown (1754) **Chariot Racing At The Ancient Olympic Games** [Photograph]. Corbis Historical via Getty Images. https://www.gettyimages.com/detail/526194946
Unknown (1754) **Early Olympics** [Photograph]. Getty Images Sport Classic. https://www.gettyimages.com/detail/51246383
Unknown (1754) **Terracotta skyphos (deep drinking cup)** [Photograph]. Universal Images Group Editorial via Getty Images. https://www.gettyimages.com/detail/1314594475
Unknown (1754) **Ancient Olympic Games, the relay race** [Photograph]. Universal Images Group Editorial via Getty Images. https://www.gettyimages.com/detail/898044534
Unknown (1900) **Bas relief of Greeks involved in various sporting (Olympics) events** [Photograph]. The LIFE Picture Collection via Getty Images. https://www.gettyimages.com/detail/50685476

Page 2

Moroz, S. (Unknown) **View On Acropolis At Sunset**, Athens, Greece [Photograph]. Shutterstock. https://www.shutterstock.com/image-photo/611816729
Unknown (2016) **Greece stock illustration** [Photograph]. kosmozoo via iStock. https://www.istockphoto.com/vector/greece-gm610139922-104671527

Page 3

Mork, A (2019) **Olympic House** [Photograph]. IOC. https://olympics.com/ioc/olympic-house
Harlingue. (1900) **Pierre de Coubertin** (1863-1937), French educator [Photograph]. Roger Viollet via Getty Images. https://www.gettyimages.com/detail/56216885

Page 4

Bicanski, M. (2017) **Lighting and Handover Ceremonies of the Olympic Flame for PyeongChang** 2018 [Photograph]. Getty Images Europe. https://www.gettyimages.com/detail/865740470

Page 5

Unknown (Unknown) **Olympic Rings** [Photograph]. IOC. https://stillmed.olympics.com/media/Images/B2B/IOC/Principles/CTA/olympic-rings-cta.jpg
Martinez, R. (2015) **Olympic rings tattoo of Andrew Gemmell** [Photograph]. Getty Images North America. https://www.gettyimages.com/detail/483494840

Page 6

Unknown (2019) **USA fans waving flags stock photo** [Photograph]. vm via iStock. https://www.istockphoto.com/photo/1126182171-296367710
Unknown (1913) **The Olympic rings** [Photograph]. IOC. https://stillmed.olympics.com/media/Images/OlympicOrg/IOC/The_Organisation/The-Olympic-Rings/Olympic_rings_TM_c_IOC_All_rights_reserved_1913.jpg
Unknown (1920) **The Olympic rings** [Photograph]. IOC. https://stillmed.olympics.com/media/Images/OlympicOrg/IOC/The_Organisation/The-Olympic-Rings/Olympic_rings_TM_c_IOC_All_rights_reserved_1920.jpg
Unknown (1957) **The Olympic rings** [Photograph]. IOC. https://stillmed.olympics.com/media/Images/OlympicOrg/IOC/The_Organisation/The-Olympic-Rings/Olympic_rings_TM_c_IOC_All_rights_reserved_1957.jpg
Unknown (1986) **The Olympic rings** [Photograph]. IOC. https://stillmed.olympics.com/media/Images/OlympicOrg/IOC/The_Organisation/The-Olympic-Rings/Olympic_rings_TM_c_IOC_All_rights_reserved_1986.jpg
Unknown (2010) **The Olympic rings** [Photograph]. IOC. https://stillmed.olympics.com/media/Images/OlympicOrg/IOC/The_Organisation/The-Olympic-Rings/Olympic_rings_TM_c_IOC_All_rights_reserved_1.jpg

Page 7

Unknown (2018) **Mt. Fuji and Tokyo skyline stock photo** [Photograph]. yongyuan via iStock. https://www.istockphoto.com/photo/904453184-249425388
Takemi, Shugo (2019) **The torch** [illustration]. Comité International Olympique. http://www.cio-pam.org/pam#Ville_TOKYO

Bicanski, M. (2017) **Lighting and Handover Ceremonies of the Olympic Flame for PyeongChang** 2018 [Photograph]. Getty Images Europe. https://www.gettyimages.com/detail/865740470

Page 8

Unknown (Unknown) **RingFAQ** [Photograph]. IOC. https://stillmed.olympics.com/media/Images/FAQ/RingFAQ.jpg
Unknown (1996) **Atlanta 1996 Torch** [Photograph] IOC via Getty Images. https://olympics.com/en/olympic-games/atlanta-1996/torch-relay
Unknown (Unknown) **Sydney 2000 Olympic Torch** [Photograph]. IOC. https://img.olympicchannel.com/images/image/private/q_auto/f_auto/q_auto/primary/rx24umwn2yqqaz8ymwda
Unknown (Unknown) **Athens 2004 Olympic Torch** [Photograph]. IOC. https://img.olympicchannel.com/images/image/private/q_auto/f_auto/q_auto/primary/d1tsvfrb2fpesdoqul1o
Unknown (Unknown) **Beijing 2008 Olympic Torch** [Photograph]. IOC. https://img.olympicchannel.com/images/image/private/q_auto/f_auto/q_auto/primary/p5yge60dluyfcmx65otx
Unknown (Unknown) **London 2012 Olympic Torch** [Photograph]. IOC. https://img.olympicchannel.com/images/image/private/q_auto/f_auto/q_auto/primary/d85m3agb99tl2ecgq34n
Unknown (Unknown) **Rio de Janeiro 2016 Olympic Torch** [Photograph]. IOC. https://img.olympicchannel.com/images/image/private/q_auto/f_auto/q_auto/primary/rwqk7gqkooyptnzayj3a

Page 9

McDermott, P. (2016) **View of Katie Ledecky's Olympic Medals** [Photograph]. Getty Images North America. https://www.gettyimages.com/detail/598880274
Tomura, A. (2019) **Tokyo 2020 Olympic Games One Year To Go** [Photograph]. Getty Images AsiaPac. https://www.gettyimages.com/detail/1163878343
Unknown (Unknown) **Athens 1896 Medal** [Photograph]. IOC. https://img.olympicchannel.com/images/image/private/q_auto/f_auto/q_auto/primary/zhb2wczydvphkbbpqopz
Unknown (Unknown) **London 1948 Medal** [Photograph]. IOC. https://img.olympicchannel.com/images/image/private/q_auto/f_auto/q_auto/primary/fo5n8vmeorax44lkqqhn
Unknown (Unknown) **Tokyo 1964 Medal** [Photograph]. IOC. https://img.olympicchannel.com/images/image/private/q_auto/f_auto/q_auto/primary/i2pivfzviagmckqiufbh
Unknown (Unknown) **Los Angeles 1984 Medal** [Photograph]. IOC. https://img.olympicchannel.com/images/image/private/q_auto/f_auto/q_auto/primary/awut8qvl5j5riib0mdlb
Unknown (Unknown) **Sydney 2000 Medal** [Photograph]. IOC. https://img.olympicchannel.com/images/image/private/q_auto/f_auto/q_auto/primary/xrpex6cdngix98gnd3tv
Unknown (Unknown) **Rio 2016 Medal** [Photograph]. IOC. https://img.olympicchannel.com/images/image/private/q_auto/f_auto/q_auto/primary/vas6aqsju204bui6hlis

Page 10

Unknown (Unknown) **Sport podium on run track under the blue sky** [Photograph]. Seksanm via Shutterstock. https://www.shutterstock.com/image-photo/1267517038

Page 11
Unknown (2021) **Musashino Forest Sport Plaza, the venue for badminton and modern pentathlon events** [Photograph]. Bloomberg via Getty Images. https://www.gettyimages.com/detail/1232062733

Page 12
Unknown (Unknown) **1972 Mascot - Munich (Waldi)** [Photograph]. IOC. https://olympics.com/en/olympic-games/munich-1972/mascot
Unknown (Unknown) **1988 Mascot - Seol (Hodori)** [Photograph]. IOC via Getty Images Europe. https://olympics.com/en/olympic-games/seoul-1988/mascot
Strahm, J. (1992) **1992 Mascot - Barcelona (Cobi)** [Photograph]. IOC. https://olympics.com/en/olympic-games/barcelona-1992/mascot
Unknown (1996) **1996 Mascot - Atlanta (Izzy)** [Photograph]. IOC. https://olympics.com/en/olympic-games/atlanta-1996/mascot
Unknown (2012) **2012 Mascot - London (Wenlock)** [Photograph]. IOC via Getty Images Europe. https://olympics.com/en/olympic-games/london-2012/mascot
Unknown (2016) **2016 Mascot - Rio De Janeiro (Vinicius)** [Photograph]. IOC via Getty Images. https://olympics.com/en/olympic-games/rio-2016/mascot
Unknown (Unknown) **1968 Mascot - Grenoble (Shuss)** [Photograph]. IOC. https://olympics.com/en/olympic-games/grenoble-1968/mascot

Page 13
Unknown (Unknown) **Motorcycle practice leaning into a fast corner on track** [Photograph]. Mark_studio via Shutterstock. https://www.shutterstock.com/image-photo/1699311712
Masae, A. (Unknown) **Virgin Island US Flag** [Photograph]. Shutterstock. https://www.shutterstock.com/image-vector/555487495
Rose, C. (2016) **Michael Phelps of the United States competes** [Photograph]. Getty Images South America. https://www.gettyimages.com/detail/589401490
Rose, C. (2016) **Ruolin Chen and Huixia Liu of China compete** [Photograph]. Getty Images South America. https://www.gettyimages.com/detail/587772216
Unknown (2014) **Water Polo Scoring Action stock photo** [Photograph]. technotr via iStock. https://www.istockphoto.com/photo/504566439-44883114
Bello, A. (2016) **Xuechen Huang and Wenyan Sun of China compete** [Photograph]. Getty Images South America. https://www.gettyimages.com/detail/589723738
Unknown (Unknown) **Triathlon Swimming** [Photograph]. IOC. https://img.olympicchannel.com/images/image/private/t_16-9_1240-700/f_auto/v1538355600/primary/v3apiecaslqb041ot58d

Page 14
Unknown (2018) **Sports Equipment on wooden background stock photo** [Photograph]. Naypong via iStock. https://www.istockphoto.com/photo/915362996-251921116

Page 16
Unknown (Unknown) **Parade of Nations** [Photograph]. IOC via Getty Images. https://olympics.com/en/news/the-remarkable-story-of-the-athletes-parade
Spencer, C. (2016) **Michael Phelps of the United States carries the flag** [Photograph]. Getty Images South America. https://www.gettyimages.com/detail/586226790

Page 17
van Hasselt, J. (2000) **Sydney 2000 - Fireworks Over Sydney Harbor** [Photograph]. Sygma. https://www.gettyimages.com/detail/542404664
Ramos, D. (2016) **Carnival dancers perform during the Closing Ceremony** [Photograph]. Getty Images South America. https://www.gettyimages.com/detail/593262668

Page 18
Unknown (2016) **Rio-Anniversary Day 16 Closing Ceremony** [Photograph]. IOC. https:/stillmed.olympics.com/media/Images/OlympicOrg/News/2017/08/21/2017-08-21-Rio-Anniversary-Day-16-Closing-Ceremony-inside-08.jpg
Spencer, C. (2016) **Eduardo Paes, IOC President Thomas Bach and Yuriko Koike** [Photograph]. Getty Images South America. https://www.gettyimages.com/detail/593259102
Unknown (Unknown) **Eiffel Tower, symbol of Paris** [Photograph]. WDG Photo via Shutterstock. https://www.shutterstock.com/image-photo/6888153

Page 21
Unknown (Unknown) **Successful concept, all gold arrows on target, archery sport** [Photograph]. Bplanet via Shutterstock. https://www.shutterstock.com/image-photo/1017417631
Alberga. (2018) **Buenos Aires Youth Olympic Games** [Photograph] World Archery. https://photos.smugmug.com/i-bCKc5X9/0/95477d8c/X4/X17_9978-X4.jpg
Gavrilovic, A. (Unknown) **Archer with medieval English longbow and arrows. Sport and recreation concept** [Photograph]. Shutterstock. https://www.shutterstock.com/image-photo/649632634
Unknown (2015) **Female archer in the field at sunset stock photo** [Photograph]. myshkovsky via iStock. https://www.istockphoto.com/photo/484131702-71354639

Page 23
Unknown (Unknown) **Competition in Synchronized Swimming** [Photograph]. Microgen via Shutterstock. https://www.shutterstock.com/image-photo/508822405
Unknown (Unknown) **Katharine Whitney Curtis** [Photograph]. Wikipedia. https://upload.wikimedia.org/wikipedia/commons/a/ad/Katharine_Whitney_Curtis.png
Unknown (1926) **Annette Kellerman** [Photograph]. Hulton Archive via Getty Images. https://www.gettyimages.com/detail/3467640
Unknown (2014) **Underwater view of synchronized swimming duet stock photo** [Photograph]. microgen via iStock. https://www.istockphoto.com/photo/502860701-44221418

Page 25
Unknown (2017) **Woman playing badminton stock photo** [Photograph]. simonkr via iStock. https://www.istockphoto.com/photo/654106828-118949183
Regan, M. (2012) **Lin Dan of China celebrates winning his Men's Singles Badminton Gold Medal** [Photograph]. Getty Images Europe. https://www.gettyimages.com/detail/149842456
Lim, E. (Unknown) **Close-Up Of White Shuttlecock Against Black Background - stock photo** [Photograph]. EyeEm via Getty Images. https://www.gettyimages.com/detail/1132509091
Boyd, R. (2017) **Shuttlecocks' sculpture** [Photograph]. Michael Ochs Archives via Getty Images. https://www.gettyimages.com/detail/836449090

Page 27
Yurlov, A. (Unknown) **Baseball players in dynamic action under sunset sky and lights of stadium** [Photograph]. Shutterstock. https://www.shutterstock.com/image-photo/1038293476
Djansezian, K. (2009) **Pedro Luis Lazo #99 of Cuba pitches** [Photograph]. Getty Images Sport. https://www.gettyimages.com/detail/85458678
McCollester, D. (2005) **Banner commemorating the Boston Red Sox** [Photograph]. Getty Images North America. https://www.gettyimages.com/detail/53028558
Courtney, N. (Unknown) **Aerial drone photo - Skyline of Denver Colorado at sunset** [Photograph]. Shutterstock. https://www.shutterstock.com/image-photo/1135691192

Page 28
Unknown (2019) **Baseball Sticker Set stock illustration** [Photograph]. bortonia via iStock. https://www.istockphoto.com/vector/1189273928-336683072

Page 29

Onischenko, E. (Unknown) **Two basketball players in action in gym panorama view** [Photograph]. Shutterstock. https://www.shutterstock.com/image-photo/232344682
Shulga, V. (Unknown) **Close up image of professional basketball player making slam dunk** [Photograph]. Shutterstock. https://www.shutterstock.com/image-photo/683804560
Unknown (1985). **Detail of the "Air Jordan" Nike shoes** [Photograph]. Focus on Sport via Getty Images. https://www.gettyimages.com/detail/53033254

Page 31

Unknown (2012) **Misty May-Treanor Wheaties Box [**Photograph]. General Mills
Schurr, S. (Unknown) **Athlete playing beach volleyball** [Photograph]. Stefan Schurr via Shutterstock. https://www.shutterstock.com/image-photo/112883197
Unknown (2015) **Beach Volleyball - a women gives a hand sign stock photo** [Photograph]. arianarama via iStock. https://www.istockphoto.com/photo/475814146-65560629

Page 33

Unknown (2012) **Muhammad Ali Wheaties Box [**Photograph]. General Mills
Hovey, J. (2021) **Navarro and team pose after tournament** [Photograph]. HoveyFilms/USA Boxing via Instagram. https://www.instagram.com/p/CNOr-8dDOHB/
Sandvik, J. (Unknown) **Close-Up Of Red Boxing Gloves Over Wooden Background - stock photo** [Photograph]. EyeEm via Getty Images. https://www.gettyimages.com/detail/713872561

Page 35

Unknown (2012) **Jon Lugball Wheaties Box [**Photograph]. General Mills
Pierse, R. (2016) **Liam Heath of Great Britain wins the gold medal in the Men's Kayak Single** [Photograph]. Getty Images South America. https://www.gettyimages.com/detail/592276148

Page 37

Unknown (2014) **Road cycling at the highest level stock photo** [Photograph]. Gorfer via iStock. https://www.istockphoto.com/photo/468663469-34230670
de Waele, T. (2020) **Mads Pedersen of Denmark and Team Trek** [Photograph]. Velo via Getty Images. https://www.gettyimages.com/detail/1273913514
Unknown (Unknown) **Cyclists - stock photo** [Photograph]. Digital Vision via Getty Images. https://www.gettyimages.com/detail/dv843023

Page 39

Unknown (2012) **Greg Louganis Wheaties Box [**Photograph]. General Mills
Dennis, A. (2012) **The judges look on as a diver competes** [Photograph]. AFP via Getty Images. https://www.gettyimages.com/detail/139414827

Page 41

Unknown (2014) **Equestrian show jumping stock photo** [Photograph]. nycshooter via iStock. https://www.istockphoto.com/photo/155907540-14986615
Sandberg, M. (2014) **Two Time Olympian Ian Miller** [Photograph]. Corbis Sport via Getty Images. https://www.gettyimages.com/detail/524956088
Unknown (Unknown) **Purebred show jumper horse canter on the race course after race** [Photograph]. acceptphoto via Shutterstock. https://www.shutterstock.com/image-photo/1583843581
Spencer, C. (2012) **Nicolas Touzaint of France riding Hildago de Lile** [Photograph]. Getty Images Europe. https://www.gettyimages.com/detail/149570079

Page 43

Didyk, A. (Unknown) **Two fencers on professional sports arena** [Photograph]. Shutterstock. https://www.shutterstock.com/image-photo/1227448015
How, H. (2016) **Fencer Mariel Zagunis poses for a portrait** [Photograph]. Getty Images North America. https://www.gettyimages.com/detail/514334800
Unknown (Unknown) **Man wearing fencing suit practicing with sword against grey vignette** [Photograph]. vectorfusionart via Shutterstock. https://www.shutterstock.com/image-photo/437171029
Unknown (1903) **Theodore Roosevelt** [Photograph]. Bettmann via Getty Images. https://www.gettyimages.com/detail/515466766

Page 45

Unknown (1932) **Greatest Hockey Player of 1928 Olympics: Dhyan Chand** [Photograph]. Bettmann via Getty Images. https://www.gettyimages.com/detail/515607960
Unknown (1908) **The British (England) Olympic hockey team** [Photograph]. Topical Press Agency via Getty Images. https://www.gettyimages.com/detail/3277353
Unknown (2003) **Zimbabwean forward Mary Campbell** [Photograph]. PIUS UTOMI EKPEI/AFP via Getty Images. https://www.gettyimages.com/detail/2577619

Page 47

Owens, M. (2021) **Danielle Kang tees off** [Photograph]. Getty Images North America. https://www.gettyimages.com/detail/1310654470
Perlstein, M. (1994) **Alan B. Shepard** [Photograph]. The LIFE Images Collection via Getty Images. https://www.gettyimages.com/detail/50475481
Unknown (Unknown) **Golf man walking with shoulder bag on course in fairway** [Photograph]. Daxiao Productions via Shutterstock. https://www.shutterstock.com/image-photo/172942391

Page 49

Unknown (2012) **Mary Lou Retton Wheaties Box [**Photograph]. General Mills
Unknown (2017) **Gymnastic equipment stock photo** [Photograph]. Polhansen via iStock. https://www.istockphoto.com/photo/865804406-143925575
Unknown (Unknown) **Still rings exercise athlete gymnast to competition in gymnastics** [Photograph]. sportpoint via Shutterstock. https://www.shutterstock.com/image-photo/709217221

Page 51

David, R. (2018) **Handball players in defence of a goal stock photo** [Photograph]. RobertoDavid via iStock. https://www.istockphoto.com/photo/1037674154-277769222
Meunier, A. (2016) **French President Francois Hollande Receives France Olympic Team At Elysee Palace** [Photograph]. Getty Images Europe. https://www.gettyimages.com/detail/594388660
Unknown (2014) **Shooting at goal. stock photo** [Photograph]. skynesher via iStock. https://www.istockphoto.com/photo/498052983-38578000
Poujoulat, A. (2021) **Switzerland's center back Andy Schmid passes the ball** [Photograph]. AFP via Getty Images. https://www.gettyimages.com/detail/1230624731

Page 53

Unknown (2018) **Two Boys Practicing Judo With Their Instructor stock photo** [Photograph]. CasarsaGuru via iStock. https://www.istockphoto.com/photo/911814002-251039523
Finney, J. (2016) **Kayla Harrison of the United States Celebrates After News** [Photograph]. Getty Images South America. https://www.gettyimages.com/detail/588550814
Nogi, K. (2021) **OLY-2020-2021-TOKYO-VENUE** [Photograph]. AFP via Getty Images. https://www.gettyimages.com/detail/1232301922
Squire, J. (2004) **Ryoko Tani of Japan celebrates winning the gold** [Photograph]. Getty Images Europe. https://www.gettyimages.com/detail/51169655

Page 55

Filimonov, I. (Unknown) **Smiling children doing karate kicks with male coach during karate class** [Photograph]. Shutterstock. https://www.shutterstock.com/image-photo/1364067908
Unknown (Unknown) **Martial arts fighters on workout in gym** [Photograph]. Nomad_Soul via Shutterstock. https://www.shutterstock.com/image-photo/1022297380
Pavone, S. (Unknown) **Okinawa, Japan at Shuri Castle** [Photograph]. Sean Pavone via Shutterstock. https://www.shutterstock.com/image-photo/733962541

Page 57

Bouroncle, C. (2019) **PANAM-2019-MODERN PENTATHLON-USA-MEX-ARG** [Photograph]. AFP via Getty Images. https://www.gettyimages.com/detail/1158417064
Unknown (1980) **Anatoly Starostin** [Photograph]. IOC. https://olympics.com/en/news/starostin-enters-modern-pentathlon-record-books
Little, W. (2016) **Announcement of Modern Pentathlon Athletes Named in Team GB for the Rio 2016** [Photograph]. Getty Images Europe. https://www.gettyimages.com/detail/538745016

Page 59

Unknown (2016) **Single Scull Rowing stock photo** [Photograph]. vgajic via iStock. https://www.istockphoto.com/photo/533718414-94558099
Scarnici, J. (2012) **U.S. Olympian Kara Kohler visits the USA House** [Photograph]. Getty Images Europe. https://www.gettyimages.com/detail/149718349
Unknown (2016) **USA celebrates with the gold medals after winning the Women's Eight Final** [Photograph]. picture alliance via Getty Images. https://www.gettyimages.com/detail/1040653824
Hangst, M. (2016) **Gold medalists United States celebrate on their boat** [Photograph]. Getty Images South America. https://www.gettyimages.com/detail/589077378

Page 61

Hyde, C. (2019) **Martin Iosefo of The United States poses for a portrait** [Photograph]. World Rugby via Getty Images. https://www.gettyimages.com/detail/1175750690
Macdougall, J. (2016) **Gold medallists Fiji celebrate during the mens rugby** [Photograph]. AFP via Getty Images. https://www.gettyimages.com/detail/588561880
Triballeau, C. (2019) **Referee Nigel Owens holds the whistle** [Photograph]. AFP via Getty Images. https://www.gettyimages.com/detail/1169386825

Page 63

Unknown (Unknown) **Regatta of sailing yachts on the sea on a windy day** [Photograph]. YanLev via Shutterstock. https://www.shutterstock.com/image-photo/664791871
West, W. (2016) **USA's Paige Railey competes in the Laser Radial Women medal race** [Photograph]. AFP via Getty Images. https://www.gettyimages.com/detail/590222878
Unknown (Unknown) **Sailing yachts regatta. Series yachts and ships** [Photograph]. Alvov via Shutterstock. https://www.shutterstock.com/image-photo/275169563
Mason, C. (2004) **Paul Foerster and Kevin Burnham of USA compete** [Photograph]. Getty Images Europe. https://www.gettyimages.com/detail/51173743

Page 65

King, B. (Unknown) **Teenage girl shooting in a shotgun competition** [Photograph]. Benjamin King via Shutterstock. https://www.shutterstock.com/image-photo/1117687877
Tucker, M. (2019) **Mary Tucker poses with gun** [Photograph]. Instagram. https://www.instagram.com/p/B2mMaHzHJcg/
Unknown (1920) **A portrait of Oscar Swahn, the oldest person to win an Olympic medal** [Photograph]. Getty Images Europe. https://www.gettyimages.com/detail/1578756
Metcalfe, M. (2020) **Australia Olympic Games Pistol & Shotgun Nomination Trials** [Photograph]. Getty Images AsiaPac. https://www.gettyimages.com/detail/1213610555

Page 67

Unknown (Unknown) **Skateboarder doing ollie on ramp** [Photograph]. guteksk7 via Shutterstock. https://www.shutterstock.com/image-photo/613801676
Unknown (Unknown) **VHS videocassette is put into the video recorder to watch the video** [Photograph]. axeiz via Shutterstock. https://www.shutterstock.com/image-photo/1079686046
Pimentel, G. (2016) **Tony Hawk Launches Tony Hawk Signature Collection** [Photograph]. WireImage via Getty Images. https://www.gettyimages.com/detail/591878008

Page 68

Eckert, E (Unknown) **Njyah Huson Maze** [Illustration]. http://www.ericjeckert.com/mazes/wp-content/uploads/2013/10/nyjah-huston1.jpg

Page 69

Unknown (2012) **US Women's National Soccer Team Wheaties Box [**Photograph]. General Mills
Unknown (2019) **Close up of good sportsmanship on the field. stock photo** [Photograph}. skynesher via iStock. https://www.istockphoto.com/photo/1154922348-314226425

Page 71

How, H. (2019) **Softball player Cat Osterman poses for a portrait** [Photograph]. Getty Images North America. https://www.gettyimages.com/detail/1189418199
Unknown (2004) **Stacey Nuveman (center) is greeted by teammates after beltin** [Photograph]. New York Daily News. https://www.gettyimages.com/detail/97314940
Unknown (1933) **Aerial View of Chicago World's Fair** [Photograph]. Bettmann via Getty Images. https://www.gettyimages.com/detail/515568368

Page 73

Colombo, C. (Unknown) **Gorges du Verdon** [Photograph]. Claudio Giovanni Colombo via Shutterstock. https://www.shutterstock.com/image-photo/367748912
Hanai, T. (2019) **Janja Garnbret of Slovenia competes in the Women Lead event** [Photograph]. Getty Images AsiaPac. https://www.gettyimages.com/detail/1168733467

Page 75

Unknown (2019) **Surfer Surfing in Poipu Beach, Kauai,Hawaii stock photo** [Photograph]. YinYang via iStock. https://www.istockphoto.com/photo/1148918112-310437018
Bielmann, B. (2020) **Two-time WSL Champion John John Florence of Hawaii is the winner** [Photograph]. World Surf League via Getty Images. https://www.gettyimages.com/detail/1230240980
Cestari, K. (2011) **Maya Gabeira of Brasil competes only to be eliminated during the Billabong Rio Pro** [Photograph]. World Surf League. https://www.gettyimages.com/detail/114142036
Chang, A. (2004) **Australian Dean Morrison riding a wave** [Photograph]. AFP via Getty Images. https://www.gettyimages.com/detail/1148310139

Page 77

Unknown (2012) **Michael Phelps Wheaties Box [**Photograph]. General Mills
Unknown (2016) **Female swimmers at swimming pool stock photo** [Photograph]. simonkr via iStock. https://www.istockphoto.com/photo/519653754-90639781
Rose, C. (2016) **Katie Ledecky of the United States competes in the Women's 800m Freestyle Final** [Photograph]. Getty Images South America. https://www.gettyimages.com/detail/589027826

Page 79

Unknown (2018) **Table tennis game stock photo** [Photograph]. South_agency via iStock. https://www.istockphoto.com/photo/930514664-255109154
Photos, C. (2004) **China's Wang Nan hits a return** [Photograph]. Getty Images AsiaPac. https://www.gettyimages.com/detail/51851947
Unknown (Unknown) **Table Tennis Player serving, motion blur, focus at the ball in the air** [Photograph]. dwphotos via Shutterstock. https://www.shutterstock.com/image-photo/1079303123
Rys, V. (2008) Guo Yue, **Wang Nan and Zhang Yining of China pose after winning the gold medal** [Photograph]. Bongarts via Getty Images. https://www.gettyimages.com/detail/82391017

Page 81

Unknown (2018) **Two girls in taekwondo combat stock photo** [Photograph]. miljko via iStock. https://www.istockphoto.com/photo/1081040008-289850469
Unknown (2019) **Hatice Kubra Ilgun (red) of Turkey competes with Anastasija Zolotic (blue) of USA** [Photograph]. Anadolu via Getty Images. https://www.gettyimages.com/detail/1186747858
Unknown (Unknown) **Two men practicing taekwondo together in the gym** [Photograph]. Freeograph via Shutterstock. https://www.shutterstock.com/image-photo/1853371705
Openshaw, M. (Unknown) **From White Belt to Black belt** [Photograph]. Madeleine Openshaw via Shutterstock. https://www.shutterstock.com/image-photo/1223763

Page 83

Unknown (2012) **Venus & Serena Williams Wheaties Box** [Photograph]. General Mills
Unknown (Unknown) **Male tennis player in action** [Photograph]. Fresnel via Shutterstock. https://www.shutterstock.com/image-photo/247251280
Brunskill, C. (2013) **Billie Jean King poses for an exclusive photoshoot** [Photograph]. Getty Images Europe. https://www.gettyimages.com/detail/171985204
Brunskill, C. (2014) **Gold medalist Andy Murray of Great Britain poses on the podium** [Photograph]. Getty Images South America. https://www.gettyimages.com/detail/589522194

Page 85

Unknown (2012) **Stacy Dragila Wheaties Box** [Photograph]. General Mills
Unknown (Unknown) **Group of multiethnic male athletics waiting at starting blocks** [Photograph]. sirtravelalot via Shutterstock. https://www.shutterstock.com/image-photo/144640133
Steele, M. (2004) **Kelly Holmes of Great Britain celebrates after she won gold** [Photograph]. Getty Images Sport Classic. https://www.gettyimages.com/detail/72477503

Page 87

Unknown (2012) **Hunter Kemper Wheaties Box** [Photograph]. General Mills
Aksonov, D. (2015) **Professional road cyclist stock photo** [Photograph]. iStock. https://www.istockphoto.com/photo/539324345-65428459
Lennon, B. (2019) **Laura Philipp of Germany celebrates winning the women's IRONMAN 70.3 Marbella** [Photograph]. Getty Images Europe. https://www.gettyimages.com/detail/1145432602

Page 89

Unknown (Unknown) **Volleyball game sport with group of girls indoor in sport arena** [Photograph]. dotshock via Shutterstock. https://www.shutterstock.com/image-photo/85071655
Haffey, S. (2016) **Karch Kiraly of the USA women's indoor volleyball team poses for a portrait** [Photograph]. Getty Images North America. https://www.gettyimages.com/detail/514337398
Unknown (Unknown) **Brown leather traditional volleyball on white background** [Photograph]. shiva3d via Shutterstock. https://www.shutterstock.com/image-illustration/1246023358
Spencer, C. (2008) **Marianne Steinbrecher #3 of Brazil tries to spike the ball past Kim Glass #10** [Photograph]. Getty Images AsiaPac. https://www.gettyimages.com/detail/82524970

Page 91

Meyers, D. (Unknown) **Water polo player throwing ball** [Photograph]. David A Meyers via Shutterstock. https://www.shutterstock.com/image-photo/1512376274
Unknown (2014) **Water Polo Scoring Action stock photo** [Photograph]. technotr via iStock. https://www.istockphoto.com/photo/504566439-44883114

Page 93

Unknown (2017) **Sportive serious people lifting barbells in gym stock photo** [Photograph]. FlamingoImages via iStock. https://www.istockphoto.com/photo/687994592-126505441
yks.media. (2020) **Delacruz mid lift** [Photograph]. Jourdan Delacruz via Instagram. https://www.instagram.com/p/CLHnjpTBHBB/
Zigic, D. (2020) **Barbell on the floor in empty health club** [Photograph]. iStock. https://www.istockphoto.com/photo/1199286507-343058977
Brunskill, C. (2016) **Lasha Talakhadze of Georgia set a new Olympic record** [Photograph]. Getty Images South America. https://www.gettyimages.com/detail/590228482

Page 95

Unknown (Unknown) **Two female wrestlers practicing** [Photograph]. Ahturner via Shutterstock. https://www.shutterstock.com/image-photo/643306588
Unknown (Unknown) **Female wrestler in a singlet and headgear**. Looking at camera [Photograph]. Ahturner via Shutterstock. https://www.shutterstock.com/image-photo/620039732
Squire, J. (2000) **Arif Abdullayev and Othmar Kuhner** [Photograph]. Getty Images Europe. https://www.gettyimages.com/detail/944150

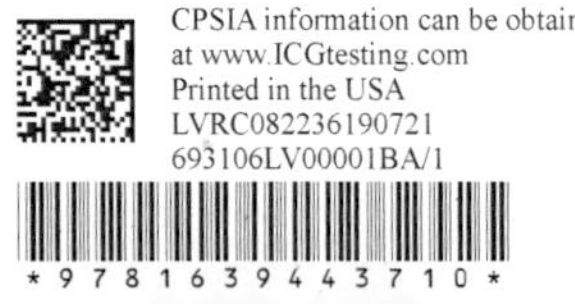

CPSIA information can be obtained
at www.ICGtesting.com
Printed in the USA
LVRC082236190721
693106LV00001BA/1

* 9 7 8 1 6 3 9 4 4 3 7 1 0 *